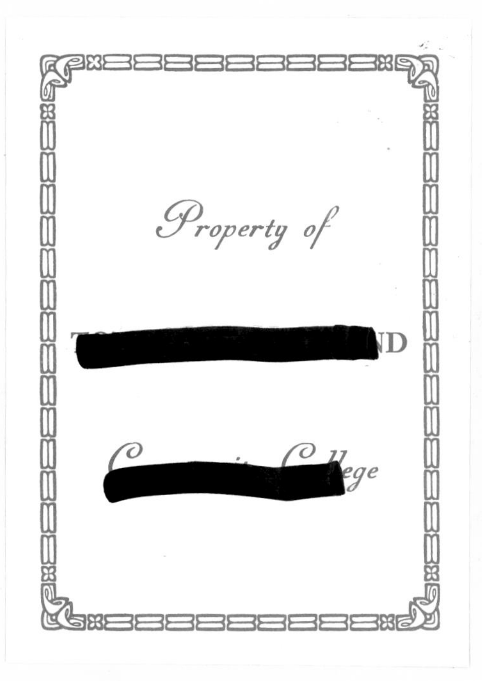
Property of

D1059815

[Louvre, Vallardi 2472, fol. 281.]

FRONTISPIECE, No. 63. Fourteen egrets.

DRAWINGS BY PISANELLO

A SELECTION
WITH INTRODUCTION & NOTES

BY GEORGE F. HILL
LATE KEEPER OF COINS AND MEDALS, BRITISH MUSEUM

DOVER PUBLICATIONS, INC., NEW YORK

Published in Canada by General Publishing Company, Ltd., 30 Lesmill Road, Don Mills, Toronto, Ontario

This Dover edition, first published in 1965, is an unabridged republication of the work first published by Les Éditions G. Van Oest, Paris and Brussels, in 1929.

The frontispiece was reproduced in color in the original edition, but appears in black-and-white in this Dover reprint.

30490

Standard Book Number: 486-21484-2

Library of Congress Catalog Card Number: 65-26653

Manufactured in the United States of America

Dover Publications, Inc.

180 Varick Street

New York, N. Y. 10014

LIST OF PLATES

Plate.	N°	Identification.		Description.
XVIII	21	— 2444	— 231	A horse, foreshortened from behind, 3/4 to l., his tail tied up.
XIX	22	— 2378	— 171	Saddled and harnessed horse, seen from behind, branded on the right hind haunch.
XX	23	— 2369	— 165	Horse lying on its side to l., the off legs drawn up.
XXI	24	— 2370	— 165	Horse lying on its side to l., all the legs extended.
XXII	25	— 2455	— 267	Forepart of a horse; two studies of the mouth, and one of the eye.
XXII	26	— 2405	— 198	Head of a horse with slit nostrils pricking its ears, seen from the front.
XXIII	27	— 2361	— 150	Head of a horse in l. profile, richly harnessed and bridled.
XXIV	28	— 2363	— 152	Head of haltered horse to r., turning slightly to front, with slit nostrils.
XXV	29	— 2360	— 149	Head of horse to front, with hanging bridle.
XXVI	30	— 2358	— 147	Head of horse to right, with hanging bridle.
XXVII	31	— 2357	— 146	Head of a horse to r., bridled.
XXVIII	32	— 2356	— 145	Head of a bridled horse in profile to r. and a foreleg.
XXIX	33	— 2355	— 144	Head of a bridled horse in l. profile.
XXX	34	— 2354	— 143	Two studies of a horses head, and one of the nose.
XXXI	35	— 2353	— 142	Four studies of horses' muzzles with slit nostrils.
XXXII	36	— 2352	— 141	Three studies of a horse's mouth and a slight sketch of the horse's chest.
XXXIII	37	— 2380	— 174	Mule, saddled, harnessed and bitted, standing to l.
XXXIV	38	— 2458	— 270	An ass standing to l., its ears laid back.
XXXIV	39	— 2493	— 237	A captive chamois.
XXXV	40	— 2489	— 234	A stag seen from behind, lying down to l., head turned away.
XXXVI	41	— 2490	— 235	Two studies of the head of a stag and the head of a doe.
XXXVII	42	— 2492	— 236	A stag standing to l.
XXXVIII	43	— 2494	— 237	Two studies of a stag, one of its head, and two guinea-fowls.
XXXVIII	44	— 2497	— 242	Young roebuck standing to r.
XXXIX	45	— 2433	— 223	Greyhound standing to r.
XL	46	— 2434	— 224	A greyhound muzzled and collared standing to l.
XLI	47	— 2435	— 225	A greyhound standing to l. wearing red collar and muzzle.

Plate.	N°	Identification.		Description.
XLII	48	— 2430	— 221	Head of greyhound to r.
XLIII	49	— 2429	— 220	Head of a hound to r.
XLIV	50	— 2423	— 215	A fox lying to l.
XLV	51	— 2424	— 215	A wolf standing to l.
XLVI	52	— 2419	— 212	A wolf or wild dog, seen from front, 3/4 l.
XLVII	53	— 2425	— 216	A cheetah ; also three twisted columns.
XLVIII	54	— 2426	— 216	A cheetah springing to r.
XLIX	55	— 2422	— 214	A cat lying to l.
L	56	— 2409	— 202	A pair of buffaloes, yoked, walking to l.
LI	57	— 2410	— 203	Cow lying down to l., about to get up.
LII	58	— 2411	— 204	Three studies of oxen lying down.
LIII	59	— 2417	— 210	A boar standing to right.
LIV	60	— 2485	— 258	Two studies of heraldic eagles.
LV	61	— 2452	— 265	A falcon, seen from behind.
LVI	62	— 2453	— 265	A falcon, with blue hood, seen from behind, perched on falconer's wrist
LVII	64	— 2450	— 263	An egret to right.
LVIII	65	— 2467	— 276	Two hoopoes.
LIX	66	— 2382	— 179	Lizard spitted through the mouth.
LX	67	— 2383	— 179	A lizard.
LXI	68	— 2419	— 212 v°	Studies of flowers.
LXII	69	— 2486	— 249	Study for a medal of Alfonso of Aragon.
LXIII	70	— 2307	— 61	Study for the 'Liberalitas' medal of Alfonso of Aragon.
LXIV	71	— 2306	— 61	Two studies for the 'Venator Intrepidus' medal of Alfonso of Aragon.

CONTENTS

PREFACE

The selection of drawings published in this volume under the name of Pisanello has been made, with few exceptions, from the wonderful series in the Louvre; and, of the Louvre drawings reproduced, all but one come from the Vallardi collection. There are indeed few drawings outside that collection which are generally admitted to the Pisanello canon; and as it is possible to obtain almost entirely from this one source a selection representative of the master, there seems to be little reason to go much farther afield.

In 1856 Giuseppe Vallardi, a Milanese publisher of prints and dealer in antiquities, brought out in Milan a catalogue of drawings in his possession, under the attribution to Leonardo da Vinci. He had acquired them, according to his statement, from a noble family in Piacenza. Such statements are notoriously untrustworthy, and this one has not enabled the earlier history of this collection to be traced. It has indeed been asserted that, in the collection in the Ambrosiana, studies by Leonardo, Cesare da Sesto, Pisanello and other masters are represented in about the same proportion as in the Vallardi collection, and it has been inferred accordingly that both collections were made at the same time and perhaps by the same collector. It may be so as regards the other masters, but it is far from true of Pisanello. For of drawings connected with him in the Ambrosiana there is a bare dozen, whereas such drawings form by far the greater proportion of the 378 sheets sold by Vallardi to the Louvre, numbering on the strictest estimate some 250.

The history of these drawings, since the time when it was discovered that so many of them were by Pisanello or his pupils and imitators, has been rather unfortunate [1]. A very natural desire to prove their connexion with the master inspired the description of an excessive number of them as « studies for » details in his pictures, although the ressemblance between, for instance, the cow in the drawing and the cow in the picture amounted to little more than this, that both were cows. That untouched drawings actually from the master's hand, drawings from which nearly all the character of the original has been eliminated by inking-over, copies by assistants or imitators, and drawings which are not in any way connected with him, even if they are of the Veronese school, were all lumped together as his work — that was perhaps inevitable then, seeing that it is, to a great degree, impossible to avoid such confusion even now. The first attempt to catalogue in detail the work of Pisanello as a draughtsman was made by Guiffrey in Venturi's edition of Vasari's *Life* (1896). But the *Catalogo dei Disegni del Pisanello* makes no pretence of discrimination between the various kinds of drawings mentioned above. The author's object was evidently to place the material before students, not to sift it. One is grateful to him for supplying a basis for all future work. It is arranged in order of folios, the *numéro d'ordre* being nevertheless placed first. Neither numeration has any classificatory significance. Some time after this list had been made it was thought advisable to break up the 'codex' and abolish the folio numeration. To find in Guiffrey-Venturi a drawing of which you do not know the obsolete folio-number now costs a considerable

1. The discovery that many of the drawings in the Recueil Vallardi are the work of Pisanello seems to have been made more or less independently by Reiset (*Gaz. d. Beaux Arts*, sér. II, t. XV, 1877, p. 119) and the Vte Both de Tauzia (*Notice des dessins de la collection His de la Salle exposés au Louvre*, 1881, pp. 60-72). Among other early publications dealing with Pisanello and chiefly inspired by these drawings, mention may be made here of the articles by Charles Ephrussi (*Gaz. d. Beaux Arts*, sér. II, t. XXIV, 1881, pp. 166-81), L. de Tauzia (*L'Art*, t. VIII (1), 1882, pp. 221-33), and Gustave Gruyer (*Gaz. d. Beaux Arts*, sér. III, t. X, 1893, pp. 353-68; t. XI, 1894, pp. 198-218; 412-27; t. XII, 1894, pp. 290-304, 485-96).

amount of search. Further, if you know the *numéro d'ordre,* you can probably find the drawing itself in the Cabinet des Dessins; but if a writer has referred to it by the folio-number only — and that, for example, is Mr. Van Marle's way — then you must first consult Guiffrey.

In 1909 a critical classification of the drawings was published as a doctoral thesis by Kurt Zoege von Manteuffel. Although this precise and painstaking author seems to depend too much on his predecessor for some details, such as measurements, he has made a careful study of the originals so far as they were accessible to him, and his list is much fuller than Guiffrey's, especially as regards drawings outside the Louvre. (If I seem to treat him chiefly as a subject for disagreement, that is because he is the only writer who has seriously attempted to discriminate among the drawings, and has therefore laid himself open to detailed criticism. Whether the present Director of the Cabinet of Prints at Dresden still holds to his classification of twenty years ago, I cannot say. « Aber », says Heine, « der Pfeil gehört nicht mehr dem Schützen, sobald er von der Sehne des Bogens fortfliegt, und das Wort gehört nicht mehr dem Sprecher, sobald es seiner Lippe entsprungen und gar durch die Presse vervielfältigt worden »).

Perhaps the most surprising thing in the history of the collection happened when the French Society for the Reproduction of Drawings by Masters undertook the publication of the drawings by Pisanello and his School preserved in the Louvre. The War interrupted the work and apparently killed the Society. In all, four portfolios containing 288 plates were issued. The promised text never appeared. The plates were numbered haphazard, presumably as they were delivered by the printer. It may be assumed that the drawings which used to be on exhibition were regarded as being among the best and most representative of the master; nevertheless few, if any, of them were included in the publication. It is poor compensation that four drawings were reproduced twice. Most disconcerting of all, there is no indication anywhere on the plates of the *numéro d'ordre* of the originals represented. Much of this, doubtless, would have been set right by an index, but for the regretted decease of the Society. Mr. Van Marle, the last to write about the drawings, complains of the difficulty of referring to them; but he himself, instead of always giving the *numéro d'ordre*, by which at least the original can be found, usually gives only the obsolete folio-number, with (in brackets) that of the reproduction in the unlucky publication just described.

Such a history looks like the work of a malignant fate, which is likely to lay its hand on any one who attempts to put things right, and involve him in some new tangle of his own. It is therefore with some tremor that, having drawn up for my own use a concordance between the *numéro d'ordre*, the old folio-number, Giraudon's list of photographs, the pages of Guiffrey-Venturi and Manteuffel, and finally the plates of the *Dessins de Pisanello et de son école*, I propose to try and persuade my long-suffering but public-spirited publisher to print it at the end of the text of this volume. If it is accurate — and where none of my predecessors, no, not one, has been impeccable in this respect, I can hardly hope to have escaped altogether — it will at least be a solid aid to future students, which is more than I venture to claim for the critical and descriptive portions of the book.

In the introduction, of the desultory character of which I am well aware, is given the briefest possible summary of the present state of our knowledge of the master's life and works. One or two problems that confront the student of his drawings are also set forth, but not solved. Aesthetic criticism, analysis of his craftsmanship, comparison with the work of other draughtsmen, have not been attempted, since I, a mere archaeologist, cannot pretend to the equipment necessary for such undertakings. I have tried to supply accurate information about details of external interest, which may help those who are competent to draw their own conclusions. But the book is not really meant for the professional student. Its object is to introduce to a wider public the work of a comparatively neglected artist, one of the keenest observers and finest delineators of men's features and animals' forms that the art of the Western world has produced.

It remains to express my obligations to those who have helped me. And naturally first of all to M. Guiffrey, for permission to photograph the drawings under his care, and to his assistant M. Rouchès; both have been unfailing in their courtesy, and will not, I hope, regard my remarks on the story of the Vallardi Collection as in any sense reflecting on themselves. M. Macon, Director of the Musée Condé, showed similar generosity to me on the occasion of a very pleasant visit to Chantilly. My colleagues of the Print Room have been unsparing of their help on all occasions when I have consulted them, at however great inconvenience to themselves; but I must more especially thank Mr. A. M. Hind, who was good enough to read and criticize the text before it reached the stage of print. At a yet earlier stage, my selection had the advantage of being submitted to the unrivalled experience of Mr. Berenson; but, while I express my gratitude for his kindness, I should like to make it clear that he is in no way responsible for any of the opinions expressed in the volume. Finally, knowing the pitfalls that beset the path of him who would identify animals and birds, I submitted many drawings to my colleagues at the Natural History Museum. They have at least saved me from confusing a sturgeon with a dolphin, a dormouse with a rat, a dog with a cat, or a hoopoe with a peewit.

The reproductions are, as far as the size of the page has permitted, of approximately the dimensions of the originals. Colour reproduction has not been attempted, except in the frontispiece, for it has been the desire of all concerned in the publication to keep it within reach of a not too swollen purse.

BRITISH MUSEUM. Jan. 1929. G. F. H.

INTRODUCTION

The life of Antonio di Bartolommeo Pisano of Verona, called Pisanello, may be read in many recent and easily accessible books [1], so that it is unnecessary here to give more than the barest summary of it.

He was born, probably at Verona, before 1395. As a young man — the date is very uncertain — he was painting in the Ducal Palace at Venice in association with or succession to Gentile da Fabriano. His earliest surviving fresco, the *Annunciation* of

1. (A) Vasari, Giorgio, *le vite de' più eccellenti pittori scultori e architettori. I. Gentile da Fabriano e il Pisanello.* A cura di Adolfo Venturi. Firenze, Sansoni, 1896. The first critical edition, with notes, documents, and reproductions, and a list of the drawings compiled by J. Guiffrey. (B) Hill, G. F., *Pisanello.* London, Duckworth, 1905. An attempt at a narrative of his life, chronology of his paintings and medals, making use of his drawings so far as they bear on his other works. This was reissued by the publishers, *unrevised*, with a new title-page dated 1911! (C) In the meanwhile, Giuseppe Biadego had discovered many important documents bearing on the artist's biography: *Atti del R. Istituto Veneto* 1907-8, t. lxvii, pp. 827 ff.; 1908-9, t. lxviii, pp. 229 ff.; 1909-10, t. lxix, pp. 183 ff., 797 ff., 1047 ff.; 1912-3, t. lxxii, pp. 1315 ff. (D) Manteuffel, Kurt Zoege von, *die Gemälde und Zeichnungen des Antonio Pisano aus Verona.* Doctoral thesis, Halle a. S., 1909. Contains a critical classification of all the drawings attributed to the master. (E) Venturi, Adolfo. *Storia dell'arte italiana,* vol. vii, Milano, 1911, 240-67. (F) Crowe, A. and Cavalcaselle, G. B., *A History of Painting in North Italy*. Ed. by T. Borenius. London, 1912, vol. ii, pp. 155-64. (G) Van Marle, Raimond, *The Development of the Italian Schools of Painting.* The Hague. Vol. viii, 1927, pp. 54-211. A very full study, especially of the paintings, with many illustrations. — It is sufficient to mention here once for all the articles by Maria Krasceninnikova in *L'Arte,* xviii, 1920, in which she attempts a classification of the drawings, apparently on the basis of the reproductions issued by the French Société de Reproduction. — As I write these words, I receive by the kindness of my friends Dr Augusto Calabi and Count Cornaggia their sumptuous work *Pisanello : l'opera medaglistica paragonata a quella pittorica distinte dalla produzione di seguaci e falsificatori dei secoli XV e XVI in relazione ai medaglioni decorativi coevi* (Milano, Modiano, 1928). The book proceeds on the same lines as the Matteo de' Pasti of the same authors, but with much greater ruthlessness. The slaughter is unexampled. Pisanello made only three medals; all the others bearing his signature are the work of forgers or imitators. The discreet student will feel that the real Pisanello has been sacrificed to an ideal (if indeed he does not call it an idol) which the authors have constructed out of their imagination. For me, they seem to be moving in an atmosphere of criticism so rarefied that I am unable to breathe in it, much less to profit by it in the present volume. — Mr. G. M. Richter's article in the *Burlington Magazine*, Aug. 1929, appeared too late for consideration here. He reproduces the *Madonna* discussed on p. 13 below.

S. Fermo, Verona, may be assigned to the period 1424-28; the evidence which has been adduced for a date some ten years later is inconclusive, and does not square with the signs of immaturity which the work presents. Pisanello's relations with Leonello d'Este began as early as 1431. In that year also and in 1432 he was painting in Rome at St John Lateran; and probably at some time between 1432 and 1438 in Florence. This period claims the *St Eustace* of the National Gallery, the *Ginevra d'Este* of the Louvre, and probably the great fresco of *St George and the Princess* in S. Anastasia, Verona. (Those who accept the later date for the fresco of the *Annunciation* must necessarily push the date of the *St George* on into the forties, i. e. between 1442 and 1448). The first medal, that of John VIII Palaeologus, was made at Ferrara in 1438. From that year until 1442 the artist was in bad odour with the Venetian Government. He had taken the side of the Gonzaga in the war of Venice against Mantua and Milan and had shown himself recalcitrant when the *fuorusciti* of Verona were allowed to come back on condition that they should reside in Padua. In November 1442 he presented himself at Venice, and obtained leave to go back to Ferrara for two months, which he did in February 1443; but Mantua and Verona were still out of bounds. Later in this year however he seems to have been permitted to revisit his native place, which hencetorward was his legal domicile.

To this troubled period, 1438 to 1443, belong the medals of Gianfrancesco Gonzaga (probably 1439), of Filippo Maria Visconti, of Niccolò Piccinino and of Francesco Sforza (1441 or 1442). From 1443 to 1448 he was busy for many patrons. Of his pictures it is probable that this period saw the painting of the *Virgin with St George and St Anthony* of the National Gallery, and the portrait of Leonello d'Este at Bergamo. The marriage medal of Leonello d'Este dates from 1444; the medals of Sigismondo and Domenico Malatesta from 1445-6; those ot Lodovico and Cecilia Gonzaga, of Vittorino da Feltre and of Belloto Cumano from 1447 and thereabouts. The medal ot Pier Candido Decembrio was finished in August 1448; then Pisanello went to Naples, where in 1449 he completed two medals of King Alfonso, and probably also that of Iñigo d'Avalos. A third medal of the King was left unsigned, and the medallist seems to have left Naples. It appears that he survived until 1455; for it is only a forced interpretation of the documentary evidence that lends support to the belief that he died earlier.

In this bare outline have been mentioned the authenticated extant works of the master; authenticated by signature or by document. The *St Eustace* is « signed all over », and the attempt of Manteuffel to assign it to an imitator has not, so far as I know, been taken seriously by any one else. On the other hand, Venturi's recent ascription to Pisanello of the *St Jerome* in the National Gallery which bears the signature of Bono da Ferrara, though it has been accepted by Van Marle, seems to me highly improbable. The management of the perspective of the receding landscape would be surprising in Pisanello, although he approaches it in the drawing of a landscape which was commonly regarded as a study for the medal of Don Iñigo d'Avalos, until Manteuffel threw doubt upon the attribution. Of the unsigned portrait in profile of a lady in Burgundian costume, now in the Clarence H. Mackay collection in America, I speak with hesitation, having seen only photographs (there is a fine reproduction in W. R. Valentiner's *Catalogue of Early Italian Paintings exhibited at the Duveen Galleries*, no. 38). We have however to reckon not only with the strikingly Northern effect of the dress (as to which it will be replied that French fashions travelled far), but with the fact that so far as we know the picture has always been in France; with the plain black background, only found in one other picture attributed, and that by mere conjecture, to this master; and with the raised gesso pattern with gilding in the hair. Comparison seems to be invited with such figures as we find in the Chaucer MS. no. 61 of Corpus Christi College, Cambridge (illustrated in *The Library*, Dec. 1925, at p. 222) or in the British Museum MS. Burney no. 25257, fol. 38 and 230. But the picture is accepted by such excellent judges that it seems impertinent to question it on purely external grounds. The attribution to the master of the profile of a man in the Capitoline Gallery, proposed by Venturi, is also highly conjectural. Finally (for we need not linger over the Berlin tondo, or the little panel of Totila before St Benedict which was some years ago in a London dealer's hands) mention must be made of a picture now in Rome which is known to me only by a photograph which I owe to the kindness of the owner and Mr Raimond Van Marle. It bears on a scroll the signature, so far as I can read it on the photograph, *Antonius Pisanus*, and represents the Virgin and Child between St John Baptist and St Catherine of Alexandria; the two saints are on a considerably smaller scale than the main figure, above which hover two angels and, higher still, the Holy Dove. The whole group is under a vine pergola, the perspective of the trellis being rather inaccurately contrived. The Virgin wears a dress lined with ermine and, so far as can be seen in the photograph, all persons represented, including the Dove, have haloes in raised gesso. If the picture with its signature is authentic, it is interesting and important, for the likeness to the work of Gentile da Fabriano is extraordinary; it is safe to say that, but for the signature, it would be attributed to that master, and not to Pisanello. In the case of other works conjecturally attributed to Pisanello's earlier period, the affinity is rather with other Veronese artists, such as Stefano da Zevio, than with the Umbrian. But since we know that Pisanello and Gentile were at one time closely associated, it would not be surprising to find traces of the affinity which is so patent here; indeed they have been observed, but never so plainly.

Let us come to the drawings. "I suppose", wrote William Bateson to his sister[1], "you didn't go to see the Old Masters' Drawings at Dresden? Perhaps there you get the very perfection of the whole thing.... When you see them, you see well enough why lots of things in pictures dont come up to scratch, simply because they were done for the world, while the man did the drawings for himself. All the drivel and halfheartedness of the pictures is away from the drawings. The fellows that did them, did them for downright love of them, and not for money or fame, as they did their pictures; and this one sees well enough in any of those drawings. And besides, too, only two or three people have ever been able to make paint shew exactly what they wanted, (and those persons have generally wanted nothing in particular!) while heaps of them could do this with chalk or bistre, and so you get to the man's real meaning at once in a drawing, while in a painting you may have to look for it through his mistakes, and often enough through a veil of tricks, which poor folks were driven to, simply to make up for absence of skill, and not always for claptrap as the brutal critics always say."

The passage is characteristic of the great naturalist's intense love of sincerity. What he says of drawings in general applies with special force to such drawings as were made without any view to an eventual painting or sculpture; for a design made with such an object in view must inevitably be hampered by the restrictions imposed by the composition for which it must serve. The artist must select, arrange, alter, omit, or add; he must not reproduce what he sees, but produce what will be serviceable to the work he is commissioned to do. Thus the "first fine careless rapture" of his inspiration is apt to evaporate. It is possible to argue that Bateson has driven his point too far; forgetting perhaps that the very power of selection and modification and arrange-

1. *William Bateson. F. R. S., Naturalist. His Essays and Addresses together with a short account of his Life,* by Beatrice Bateson. Cambridge, 1928, pp. 23-4.

ment of what the artist's eye first sees in the natural objects is the secret of the superiority of his vision over the unintelligent perception of the ordinary man. A great work of art, completed, is something to make which all these preliminary studies have been purged of their inessentials, their spirit distilled in the alembic of their maker's imagination, to combine at last in some serene and radiant vision of the idea which was hidden from earthly gaze until genius revealed it. But it is only the greatest artists who can carry such a matter to its conclusion without losing the freshness of the first inspiration. So that the power to do so becomes a test of greatness, and we can judge clearly, in the example before us, how much greater the man was as a medallist than as a painter. Looking at his finest medals, we tread on the very heights of art; in this keen but tranquil air there arises no desire to analyse or explain, they inspire the same quiet thrill of wonder after many years as on the first day we beheld them. His paintings, especially his larger compositions, though they have interest, charm and beauty, are composed of elements which are imperfectly blended; they go to pieces as we gaze, lovely fragments indeed, but fragments which could be combined, we feel, equally well in other ways. But looking at his drawings we have none of that uneasy feeling that, delightful and amusing as the whole may be in its way, many parts of it might be left out without detriment to the general idea. The exceptions to this rule are instructive; they are drawings made in deliberate preparation for some composition — most instructive of all, perhaps, the design for the obverse of the "Liberalitas Augusta" medal of Alfonso of Aragon. The description given below of Pl. LXIII will shew how in the completed medal inessentials have been removed and the whole design simplified and dignified. But would quite so much of the quaint and amusing have been sacrificed in a painting? Nevertheless another example may serve to shew how even in a fresco he learned to sow with the hand and not with the sack. Consider the studies of hanging corpses (Pl. XIII). Two of them were used for the gallows detail in the completed fresco in S. Anastasia; but where a Low Countries painter would probably have chosen the most gruesome of the three victims, this has been deliberately avoided by the Italian. It is not a question of "good taste" or "refinement", which are responsible for more banalities than anything else in art; it is simply that the intrusion of this decaying corpse, with mouth agape, eyes dribbling corruption, and beard of some days' growth, into the scene of St George departing for the fray, would have sounded a note too violently jarring. The ghastly details were doubtless reserved for the monster's den, now effaced by time.

Natural beasts were, of course, made to supply ideas for the fictitious monsters of legend, and it was reasonable to make a goat pose for a unicorn (the unicorn of the medal of Cecilia Gonzaga is certainly studied from a goat, even though the goat in the Chatsworth Collection be not by Pisanello); but it may be doubted if it ever occurred to any other artist to spit a wretched lizard and make him do duty for the dragon of St George (Pl. LIX).

Such as we have them, the drawings by Pisanello, or attributed to him, fall into certain groups. From the point of view of technique, they employ the materials and tools usual at the time : pen or brush; ink, bistre, or other browns [1] and watercolour; chalk, and silverpoint; all these used on paper or parchment. The paper on which an extensive series of drawings survives has been reddened. It is held by Manteuffel that these drawings, in their present condition for the most part very coarse and retaining practically nothing of the master's actual workmanship, are transfer drawings for fresco-work. Where they can be definitely connected with extant frescoes (as is the case with Pl. XIV) they correspond, he maintains, in dimensions. He reconstructs the process as follows; the original study, which was probably on a smaller scale, was redrawn either by the master himself or by a pupil on the scale of the fresco, then gone over with red chalk and pressed on the wet plaster, where it appeared in the reversed sense. In this process the drawing was naturally liable to become blurred and spoiled; but it would seem that pious pupils went over them again with ink. Assuming that Manteuffel's statement about the dimensions is exact — a matter which seems to require some verification — we might accept his theory if an explanation of two other facts were forthcoming. In the first place, the drawings and the portions of the fresco to which they correspond should always be in opposite senses. That is so with the drawing of the head of the princess of the S. Anastasia fresco already referred to. But it is not so with the head of the Oriental, who is second from the left, that is, next to the Kalmuck, in the group of riders. The drawing (Pl. 109 in the *Dessins*, Pl. 21 in my *Pisanello*) shews the head in the same position [2]. A still more serious objection is that these are not, if they ever were, drawings in red chalk on *white* paper. The whole sheet has been reddened. If that was done before pressing the

1. Apparently not sepia, which, if Meder is right, was not in use at that time.

2. There is, so far as I know, no trace, in any of the drawings with which we are concerned, of pricking or pressing a sharp point along the lines, which would shew that they had been used for transferring the outlines, in the same sense and not in reverse, to another round.

sheet on the wet plaster, all that it would produce would be a formless red patch. If it was done afterwards, why was it done? Was it because the original red line, under the influence of the damp, had " spewed ", so that when the pious pupil went over it with ink he could not cover it, but an ugly irregular margin of red remained on each side of his pen-line, to remove the effect of which he proceeded to redden the whole sheet? But then why was such a sheet as that on Pl. IV, which could never on any supposition have been used as a transfer, bearing as it does a mere rough sketch, treated with the same piety? The same question must be asked of the two landscape sketches in no. 2594 on fol. 100 verso (*Dessins*, no. 21). Was it because the red went through from one side to the other of the paper, so that both sides, to save appearances, had to receive a complete covering of red? The problem is sufficiently interesting to call for suggestions in support of the only explanation that has been offered, unsatisfactory though it may seem to be.

Before leaving the subject of materials, a word may be said about watermarks. In spite of the doubts which some critics entertain about the value of the study of these marks, there is something to be done with them, provided it is understood that the evidence which they furnish is only of a confirmatory character. It is obvious that if the paper on which drawings of doubtful attribution are made can be shown to be the same as that used for drawings admittedly genuine, one point in favour of the former is gained. And conversely, if the mark on the paper of a doubtful drawing is not known to appear on the paper of any that are accepted as genuine, its claim to genuineness is weakened. For the present, I put on record notes of the three marks most frequently found on the drawings of Pisanello and his school.

First there is a Moor's head bound with a diadem — as on the arms of Pucci of Florence. I have observed it on sixteen folios of the Vallardi Collection [1]. That no less than eleven of these sheets were used by Pisanello is admitted by all those who have studied him with care. In cases of doubt, the presence of this mark, or the identification of the paper as of the same make, although the mark may not have survived, must surely weigh a trifle in favour of acceptance.

1. Folio 55 (no. 2299); 80 (2478); 141 (2352); 142 (2353); 146 (2357); 147 (2358); 148 (2359); 152 (2363); 161 (2366); 165 (2370); 169 (2375); 234 (2489); 263 (2450); 265 (2453); 276 (2466, 2467); 278 (2469). Of these, nos. 2370, 2363, 2358, 2357, 2353, 2352, 2489, 2453, 2450, 2467 are reproduced on Plates xxi, xxiv, xxvi, xxvii, xxxi, xxxii, xxxv, Lvi, Lvii, Lviii of the present volume.

Another common mark is a pig standing to the right [1]. It is found on seventeen folios. Of these only two are admitted by Manteuffel. By far the greater number are indeed coarse drawings, and the paper has been reddened in the way already described. The probability is that it was used in Pisanello's workshop, but chiefly for rough work, and for drawings which were afterwards inked over by assistants, whether they were originally the work of the master or not.

The third mark, the triple mount, is found on only eight folios [2], of which only one seems to have much claim to association with Pisanello [3].

More body needs to be given to this evidence, by comparison of sheets on which the mark has not been preserved with those on which it has; but the notes just given are enough to show that the evidence is worth collecting, where every scrap is precious.

To return to the subject of the master's technique. That a certain amount of the watercolour that appears on these drawings is hardly from his own brush — unless we admit that he sometimes used it like a child — is beyond doubt. But many of the finest watercolours have been excluded by Manteuffel on technical grounds. Such is the lovely pointer's head which is reproduced — but not, alas! in colour — on Pl. XLIII. As the technical reasons for rejecting them are liable to misinterpretation in a translation, I think it desirable to give the original German. « Alle sind sie aber zuerst mit einem sehr weichen Stift nicht nur angelegt, sondern auch modelliert, und zwar durch Wischen. Ganz deutlich ist dies Verfahren bei den unkolorierten Blättern zu erkennen, aber auch bei den nachträglich aquarellierten sieht man die ursprüngliche Anlage überall, wo keine Farbe aufgetragen ist oder sie nur sehr dünn liegt. Jenes Trennen von Farbangabe und Modellierung, wie überhaupt das Verwischende und Fleckenhafte des Auftrags, widerspricht der Art Pisanos und überhaupt der des Quattrocento

1. 22 (2278); 38 (2281); 103 (2597); 104 (2598); 105 (2599); 106 (2600); 110 (2604); 114 (2607); 117 (2610); 120 (2613); 124 (2617); 125 (2618); 126 (2619); 128 (2621); 129 (2622). Of the same kind of paper are 20 (2276) and 21 (2277). There are reproductions of nos. 2276-2278 in this volume on Plates VII-IX.

2. 10 (2264); 11 (2266); ? (2271); 37 (2280); 64 (2315); 137 (2626); 251 (2507); 260 (2515). It is given by Briquet, p. 102, as being in use from 1356 to 1461.

3. Among these is the drawing of a landscape, already referred to, which has usually been connected with the medal of Don Iñigo d'Avalos (no. 2280), but to which Manteuffel has raised objection on the ground of the treatment of perspective. I must confess that a fresh examination of the drawing confirms my original belief in Pisanello's authorship.

vollständig". That is to say, the original drawing is made with a very soft point, not only for the first sketch but to finish the modelling, using the point as one uses a stump with charcoal. It can be seen even under the subsequently applied colour where that is not too thick. This separation of colouring from modelling, and the blurred and patchy character of the applied colour, are altogether contrary to the manner of Pisanello and of the Quattrocento generally. — It would have been easier to control Manteuffel's argument had he brought in evidence other datable watercolours which supported his exclusion of these from the master's work and indeed from his period. To say vaguely that the drawing of mice (no. 2387, fol. 183, *Dessins*, no. 198 — they are really dormice, *glis glis*) shews a discontinuity of line and a pictorial conception ("ein Absetzen des Striches und eine malerische Auffassung") which may indicate the sixteenth century, does not carry conviction.

Where a professional critic may so easily fail to justify his verdicts, it were rash in me to give reasons for all the categories which I have excluded. A few observations may however be ventured. One of the most remarkable drawings in the Vallardi Collection is the beautiful profile bust of a woman with her left hand raised, done in bistre on parchment (no. 2344; Giraudon 12106; Müntz, *Hist. de l'Art pendant la Renaissánce*, I, at p. 638). Although it is still attributed to Pisanello in the Cabinet des Dessins, neither Guiffrey nor Manteuffel mentions this; why then, it may be asked, drag it in at all? The answer is that it appears to be by the same hand as the tonsured head in profile (no. 2329, fol. 72; *Dessins*, no. 102), in pen and silverpoint on parchment, which has generally, except by Manteuffel, been accepted as Pisanello's work. Both are finished in exactly the same delicate way with touches of watercolour, on lips, inside of ear, nostrils and eyes in the first case, on lips cheek and ear in the second. The bust of the woman, with narrow, small eye under a highly arched eyebrow, with lightly opened lips, recalls the frescoes of the Oratory of Saint George at Padua. The stiff pose of the arm, which hardly looks as if it belongs to the body, is not out of keeping with such a date. Fol. 71, no. 2328 (*Dessins*, no. 223) perhaps belongs to the same group.

There is a group of drawings in black chalk, of which Dr J. P. Richter once told me that he considered them to be early and to show the influence of Altichiero. There could hardly be anything more unlike the drawings just mentioned. Manteuffel relegates them to the end of the fifteenth century. They are nos. 2335 to 2338 (*Dessins*, nos. 242, 107, 224 and 24). All of them are of old men, nos. 2335 and 2337 of one, 2336 and 2338 of another old man. On the *verso* of the last is the hardly visible and usually ignored sketch of a gentleman holding a stick in both hands (*Dessins*, no. 22). If these are not by Pisanello, neither are they, as it once seemed to me they were, to be connected with the profile head of a bearded man, wearing across his breast a cord fastened by a ring surmounted by a cross (no. 2339). This head, which Van Marle describes as one of Pisanello's finest drawings, has been in any case ruined by retouching of the profile and various details. Whether it is by Pisanello one may hesitate to say, and some might call it a dull drawing. But it has another interest, in the colour notes written against the beard.

These colour notes raise the whole question of the handwriting of Pisanello, a question which has never been squarely faced by any of his biographers. Cursive script occurs on the following drawings by or associated with the master :

a) Louvre, 2274. Pen on parchment 8,5 × 6,6 cm.

An ornament consisting of two interlaced gothic letters (*a* and *o*) suspended by a chain from a twig passed through two holes in a garment. The script appears to read *Jabus (quon)dam dns Micha.*

b) Louvre 2470, f. 279 (*Dessins*, 287). Against one of the birds is written *Grachalo. Gracolo* is another name for the *gracchia* or chough, but this bird is no chough. Mr. P. R. Lowe of the Natural History Museum identifies it from a photograph of the drawing as undoubtedly a Bearded Vulture (*Gypaëtus barbatus*).

c) Louvre, 2339, f. 86 (*Dessins,* 31; a fine reproduction in Van Marle at p. 180). Against the beard is writen *piu chanuta* and *canuta*, indicating that the hair is to be " more white " and " white ".

d) Louvre 2391, fol. 189 (Giraudon, 12212). Studies of sixmonkeys and a sturgeon. Written against the last is the word *addano* [1].

e) Louvre M. I. 1062 (*Dessins*, 72). On the much discussed drawing of studies for an Emperor, probably John VIII Palaeologus, on horseback, and other subjects, the following colour notes occur : (i) *azuro* and *oro* on the ground and lettering of the Arabic inscription. (ii) *el rouesso del vestj rosso | el chapello turchin fodrado de pance de*

1. As to this Prof. Foligno writes : " *Adano* = Ital. *adello* (also *adeno*) a sea-fish which seems to have at certain times proceeded up the river Po (it was called *ledano* in the Polesine); I don't think such a fish is to be met with in the Po now; it was a kind of sturgeon with a more yellowish skin. Dictionaries add : *acipenser huso* of Linnaeus ; *attilus* in Pliny ". *A. huso* is the giant sturgeon ; but the fish in this drawing is identified by the Natural History Museum as *A. sturio*, the common sturgeon.

varo | li stiuali de chuoro zallo smorto | la guaina del larcho bizaca e grenelossa e cosi quella de turcasso e de la simitarra. (iii) *Lo chapelo de linperadore sie biancho dessoura | e rouersso rosso el profilo da torno nero la zupa verde | de dalmascin e la gona de soura de chermezin [?]ede la | facia palida la barpa negra chapelj e cilgij el simile | hochi grizy e tra in verde e chine le spale picholo di p(er)sona.* I. e. (i) The lettering is to be gold on a blue ground. (ii) The back of the dress red, the hat turquoise blue lined with bellies of vair, the boots of pale yellow leather, the bow-case ashen-gray [1] and grained, and so also the quiver and the sheath of the scimitar. (iii) The hat of the Emperor to be white above, the back red, the edge of the brim black, the coat green, of damask, the shirt over crimson... the face pale, the beard black, hair and eyebrows the same, eyes gray to green, shoulders bent, stature small.

The handwriting of the scripts *c*, *d*, and *e* is almost certainly the same. As to the dialect of *e*, Prof. Cesare Foligno informs me that it belongs to ' Venetia' rather than to 'Venice,' and "the writer was clearly endeavouring to use a 'literary' language and did so by furbishing up his own vernacular. He was only so far successful as to make it impossible to localise his dialect beyond saying that it belonged to Venetia." It follows that we cannot argue from the inscription to a Venetian origin for the drawing.

f) Collection of Mr. F. Lugt (Maartensdijk, Utrecht). Reproduced by Venturi in *L'Arte*, 1925, p. 36, and by Van Marle, fig. 63. A courtier paying his respects to a lady. Above, the following doggerel :

O nobilisima dona Adornata de oni belece
vaga siete nei vostri bei senbia(n)tij
posto che sia tanta la vostra nobilita in altece
che a tuti no(n) sia possibile Co(m)p(r)e(n)de(re)? e vostri vagi pe(n)sieri tanti
ma io come sperato dal dio d'amore (con) so Asperece
non o potuto far dimeno ch' io no(n) ischriua(?) qua(n)ti
E quali sono le mie inumirabile pene ch'i(o) porta
dicho per te madona che sei tuta torta

Below in a different hand :

Onor vi' o fato e fazo
p(er) poder star (con) vuy in solazo.

1. *Bizaca* I have translated as above; Prof. Cesare Foligno also thinks that it seems to go back to

Of these two inscriptions, the second, according to information from the owner, is in slightly darker ink than the drawing, and may have been added a little later; the former is in the same ink as the drawing, and was doubtless written at the time. As to the language, Prof. Foligno writes : « the spellings 'beleçe, alteçe, aspereçe' (I add the cedilla, for it was often overlooked by scribes) postulate a North Italian writer, a Lombard or a Venetian for choice »

We thus have on the drawings five different handwritings (*c*, *d*, and *e* being the same and *f* providing two varieties), one of which may belong to the master. A sixth is given by the mysterious signature which was in the Fillon collection and has since disappeared. This last looks on the face of it extremely dubious, and is probably a mystification. The occurrence of three examples of the same hand on three different sheets is certainly presumptive evidence that it is the master's, provided that the three drawings are to be considered authentic. But the drawing of *e* has always seemed to me more in the Venetian tradition than in Pisanello's manner. Of *c*, which Müntz thought might be an early work, a study for the fresco in the Ducal Palace, Manteuffel remarks that this cannot be proved any more than it can for the other studies which Müntz proposed to connect with the same fresco. He has however failed to notice that the person represented wears on his coat a chain and a badge which suggests the Imperial *globus cruciger*. There is therefore some reason to suppose that the man belonged to an Imperial suite, just as the horse in no. 2378 (pl. XIX) may have belonged to an Imperial stable, since it is branded with the same mark. At the same time there is something to be said for dissociating this drawing from Pisanello; as Manteuffel remarks, it is too small and timid in style, with a smallness, be it added, which is not that which is observable in certain immature works generally accepted as his. As to *d*, it is dismissed by Manteuffel as a pupil's work. Now if these three drawings are by two or three different hands, how comes it that the same person wrote notes on them all? If they were all pupils of one man, there is no difficulty. It looks therefore as if we should have to accept the drawing *e* in spite of its Venetian affinities, as the work of a pupil. The conclusion is, I admit, somewhat halfhearted; but at any rate the materials for a more satisfactory solution, if one is possible, are now before the student.

bizo (bigio) and thus *bizaca* (bizaça) = *bigiaccia* = grayish ; " this form is however unconvincing and leaves one hesitating ".

Is it possible to arrange the drawings in any sort of chronological order? Here again, it is to be feared, the answer must be rather vague. If only the paintings were certainly dated, we should have *termini ante quos* for a number of drawings, which were certainly in existence before the paintings. But they need not have been made immediately before the paintings; Pisanello must constantly have been referring to old sketchbooks. As Van Marle observes, he "made drawings and sketches of everything he found interesting and when he had an order for a picture he fell back on his sketch books and represented in his painting, apart from the actual subject, anything that happened to please him. Even the principal subjects, I think, must often have taken the appearance suggested to the artist by the sketches made at quite another time and when the artist did not yet know to what future use he would put them."

On the other hand there are a few drawings which can be dated with a fair amount of certainty. The latest are those which are connected with Alfonso of Aragon; they belong to the latter part of 1448 and 1449, and some of them actually bear these dates. A very interesting set of designs for plate (saltcellars) in the shape of dragon-borne ships, and for bombards, are, the former perhaps, the latter certainly, of Neapolitan origin, and the same is true of some small designs for medals and coins; unfortunately these are all too coarse to find a place in Pisanello's works, though they may well be by pupils of his. The watermark of two of the sheets with implements of war is a cinquefoil, not otherwise found in drawings attributed to Pisanello; the marks on the paper used for the salts are unfortunately obscure, but, so far as they can be made out, they too do not occur on paper known to have been used by him. There is thus little remaining in the way of drawings from his Neapolitan period. On the other hand, if we go back to the period 1438 to 1442 we may date with certainty the profile sketch of the head of John VIII Palaeologus (no. 2478, fol. 80), unfortunately too faint to repay reproduction, although that has been attempted in Calabi and Cornaggia's book. It must date from 1438, whether it was made for the medal or for a panel portrait. For, one may remark in passing, Pisanello was first of all a portrait-painter, and probably first painted portraits of most of those people whose features he afterwards rendered in the less perishable form of medals. Thus the studies of Niccolò Piccinino (Pl. XI) and Filippo Maria Visconti (nos. 2483, fol. 88 and 2484, fol. 89, *Dessins*, nos. 32 and 206; of which the second is certainly not, the first not certainly, an original work of the master) are to be associated in the first instance with paintings now lost, rather than with the medals which they so closely resemble in everything but shape. However this may be, here again is a group datable, in all probability, to the time when the medals were made, 1441 or thereabouts.

I must confess to complete uncertainty about the date of the great mass of the animal studies. An inclination to put most of them rather early is perhaps inspired by the belief already stated above that the fresco of S. Anastasia, which so many of them evidently precede, is before 1438 rather than after 1442.

One early group of drawings seems to be that which shews the inspiration of the antique. The group is represented in the present volume by plates I. II. To these must be added the boarhunt at Berlin, no. 1358, from a sarcophagus; and a copy of the Tiber (or as it then was the Tigris) of the Capitol, also at Berlin (1359 verso); the two Bacchants of Oxford (Colvin II, Pl. 27 verso); and various others, which I have discussed elsewhere. (Possibly also the study in the Louvre (06949) of young men breaking sticks.) The Bacchants shew more mastery of the human form, and may perhaps come late in the thirties; the others, by the curiously stiff, angular, and rather timid drawing of the nude, and their imperfectly understood anatomy, take us some years farther back, perhaps to the time when Pisanello was working in Rome in 1431-2, and might have seen the Adonis sarcophagus which interested him. It is only fair to mention that Manteuffel will have none of these drawings, except perhaps that at Oxford, which he has not seen.

In the circumstances I have not felt justified in attempting more than a very loose classification of the selection published here. The drawings inspired by the antique have been placed first. There follow a few designs for compositions and portraits which are at any rate not late; they seem to be mostly connected with Ferrara and Mantua before 1442. Next come studies more or less definitely associated with the fresco of S. Anastasia. These lead on to the important series of animal studies, which are classified according to subjects, though for lack of space not all the kinds of animals that attracted the master's pencil are represented : some will miss his amusing monkeys. One sheet of flower-studies follows; and finally the designs for medals of Alfonso of Aragon.

And, if the selection were to be made again, the riches are such that it would be possible to do it without much repetition. That may serve to meet the criticism that it might have been better done.

DESCRIPTION OF THE PLATES

FRONTISPIECE

See **Nº 63**.

PLATE I

Nº 1. — Louvre, Vallardi, 2397 fol. 194 verso.

Pen on parchment. 19.5 × 27.2 cm.

Nude figures from the antique. (1) On the right, a young man wielding a club, a cloak hanging over his left arm. This is a misunderstood rendering, the right arm and the club being an addition by the artist, of a figure of Orestes on a sarcophagus, perhaps that which was in the Palazzo Giustiniani, and which was used by Raphael, or one now in the Cathedral at Husillos near Palencia. (2) Seminude female figure moving to the right; copied from the Venus on an Adonis sarcophagus which is known to have been at Rome in the sixteenth century and is now at Mantua. (3) Youth kneeling to front, from an antique model not traced.

On the recto, a pen study of a goat's head, and one of the whole animal on a smaller scale (Gir., 12224. *Dessins*, 126).

In very much the same style as the studies on the verso is a boarhunt scene on a sheet at Berlin (no. 1358; *Papers of the Brit. Sch. at Rome*, iii, 1906, p. 302 and Pl. XXXI 2; Mant., p. 168), probably from the same Adonis sarcophagus.

Gir., 12168. *L'Art*, VIII (1), 1882, p. 227; Vent., p. 108; Hill, *Papers of the Brit. Sch. at Rome*, III, 1906, p. 301 and Pl. XXXII; *Dessins*, 20; Mant., p. 155; Marle, p. 155, fig. 93.

PLATE II

Nº 2. — British Museum, P. p. 11, verso. From the Lagoy Coll.

Pen (over chalk) on parchment. 16.5 × 23.5 cm.

Two allegorical figures: a nearly nude bearded man, wearing a wreath of leaves (ivy?) holding over his shoulder a vulture which is vomiting; and a nude figure of a woman (Truth or Vanity) holding up a mirror. Timid drawing, and presumably an early work. The indirect influence of the antique is obvious. The head of the nude woman is found copied on a large scale in a coarse hand on reddened paper in Vallardi, no. 2589, fol. 94 verso (Gir., 12110, *Dessins*, 182; watermark *stag*).

On the recto are two chalk studies of heads, a man and a woman.

Hill, *Pisanello*, p. 239; Hind, in L'*Arte*, viii, 1905, p. 210; Ricketts, in *Vasari Society*, i, 1905-6, nos 11(verso) and 10 (recto); Mant., p. 170.

PLATE III

N° 3. — Louvre, Vallardi, 2631, fol. 157 verso. Pen on reddened paper (no watermark). 25.2 × 37.7 cm.

On the left half of the sheet (or rather, on the left of two sheets joined together), a horse's head (not reproduced). On the right a number of studies, as follows: — Upper portion, left : design for filling the right-hand spandril of an arch; four seated figures, three of which are doubtless evangelists; two of them are at desks. The fourth figure, nearest the arch, appears to be reading a book, and the arrangement with an animal lying below recalls the Virgin's side of the *Annunciation* of San Fermo. To the right of this scheme is a kneeling angel of the Annunciation, a very spirited light sketch, and a rather more detailed study of drapery lying over something (knees of a seated figure ?). Further to the right, the symbols of the four Evangelists; among them, more faintly shown, a figure (according to Van Marle, an angel swinging a censer; but I can see no wings). In the middle of the page, a composition for an altar-piece : the Virgin enthroned to front, the Child on her lap; on her right St Anthony Abbot and a saintly monk holding the model of a church; on her left, a warrior saint in armour (St George, probably) and St Catherine of Alexandria. Finally, in the right-hand bottom corner, a very slight sketch of a *Crucifixion*, with the Virgin, St Mary Magdalene at the foot of the Cross, and St John. A puzzling feature of the sheet is the series of dots and dashes, the latter arranged in sets of four lines. They bear no relation to the drawings, or one might say that they indicated the position of the text on a page to be illuminated.

The coincidence of three of the five figures in the centre composition with those of the *St Anthony and St George* of the National Gallery suggested to me that this might embody a first idea for that picture. To argue, as Manteuflel does, that it cannot be a " study for " the picture because it has not the characteristic arrangement finally adopted is to assume that an artist never considers more than one arrangement before he decides on his final scheme. The drawing is, in any case, important as being the most elaborate of the very few by Pisanello which contain plans for larger compositions.

On the recto of the sheet, two horses' heads, one in profile to the left, the other to front (Gir., 12200).

Gir., 12165; Vent. p. 103; Hill p. 47, p. 157; Mant., p. 138; *Dessins*, 273; Marle, p. 156, and fig. 95.

PLATE IV

N° 4. — Louvre, Vallardi, 2595, fol. 101 verso. Pen on reddened paper (no water mark). 25.8 × 19 cm.

A party riding out into the country. The drawing would seem to have some connexion with the medal of Gianfrancesco Gonzaga; compare the chief riding figure and the armed page seen from behind on the extreme right, with those on the medal. That it was made with a view to medallic design is of course unlikely; it recalls rather frescoes of court occupations such as have survived in the Schifanoia Palace at Ferrara or in the Chapel of Queen Theodolinda at Monza. But that the idea which it represents was afterwards used for the medal it is not unreasonable to suppose. In one particular the drawing has generally been misinterpreted; the lady, be she Cecilia Gonzaga or another, is not riding but standing on the ground; there is no sign of any horse for her, and her long train sweeps the ground, being thrown forward just like that of the Princess in the fresco of St Anastasia. The drawing which is compared with this by Heiss (*Vittore Pisano*, p. 24) and stated to be at Oxford, is in the Ambrosiana, and is merely a copy after the medal; see Manteuffel p. 171-2, who corrects the various confusions into which others have fallen about this drawing.

On the recto (*Dessins*, 13) a man's head facing, with eyes closed and mouth open (cp. no. 2594, fol. 100 recto).

Gir., 12160; Heiss, p. 23; Vent., p. 98; Hill, p. 170 and Pl. 50; Mant., p. 134; *Dessins*, 19; Marle, fig. 120; *L'Arte*, 1920, p. 17.

PLATE V

N° 5. — Louvre, Vallardi, 2432, fol. 219. Pen on reddened paper (no watermark). 25 × 18 cm.

Studies of dogs, and the heads of a pair of greyhounds; these summarily sketched a second time below. On the right, a vacant space has been used for a very rapid sketch of an audience in a hall with battlements and arched windows; within, a person seated on a dais, another person standing beside him, a figure kneeling before him, and four rows of people seated. The way in which the edges of this sketch are broken by the contours of two of the dogs indicates that it was placed on the paper subsequently to the studies of dogs, which do not look like early work. It follows that it is not a sketch for, much less after, the fresco in the Ducal Palace at Venice.

On the verso are studies of the head and forelegs of a spaniel, inked probably by a later hand, and anyhow quite spoilt.

Gir., 12230; Wickhoff in *Repertorium für Kunstwissenschaft*, vi, 1883, pp. 20f; Müntz in *Rev. de l'art anc. et mod.*, i, 1897, p. 69; Vent., p. 111; Hill, p. 31, pl. 5; Mant., p. 133; *Dessins*, 67; Marle, p. 67-8. Verso: Gir. 12227; *Dessins*, 40.

PLATE VI

N° 6. — Louvre, Vallardi, 2398, fol. 195. Pen on parchment. 17.6 × 22.7 cm.

Various studies: two devils, with bats' wings and long tails; a pelican in her piety; two studies for the Virgin reading in a book; a golden eagle perched on an open book; a dromedary with a rider of whom only one leg is indicated *behind* the hump; and a small bear holding a goose in his jaws.

The attempts which have been made to connect some of the drawings on this sheet with various paintings and medals are even less convincing than usual (see Manteuffel's judicious remarks). The pelican in her piety for instance has no special connexion with the medal of Vittorino da Feltre, but is part of the common stock in trade of the artist of the time; the renderings of the subject in drawing and medal are quite different. The posing of the eagle on an open book is either meant for an *impresa*, though it seems to have nothing to do with Alfonso of Aragon (indeed the drawing looks earlier than 1448): or it may be an idea for the symbol of St John the Evangelist.

Gir., 12156; *Gaz. des Beaux Arts*, III, xii, 1894, p. 493; Heiss, p. 27; Vent., p. 109; Hill, p. 205; Mant., p. 124; *Dessins*, 18.

PLATE VII

N° 7. — Louvre, Vallardi, 2276, fol. 20. Pen on gray paper (no watermark). 20. 8 × 14.3 cm.

Studies of Venetian gothic architecture; in the corner, profile portrait to left of Niccolò III d'Este, in elaborate cap.

By Ephrussi and Guiffrey this portrait has been taken for Gianfrancesco Gonzaga, by myself, Manteuffel and Van Marle for Niccolò d'Este. The rendering of the lower part of the face is exactly like that on the medals of Niccolò. Compare also the portraits on Pl. X.

It is however only fair to say that, since this drawing is connected by the paper on which it is drawn with nos. 2277 and 2278, of which the latter is certainly associated, by the coat of arms, with the Gonzaga, we obtain more unity in the group by identifying the portrait on this sheet, and consequently that on the His de la Salle sheet, Pl. X, as Gianfrancesco Gonzaga. The conclusion is not however inevitable, seeing that Pisanello was evidently working for both patrons about the time that these drawings must have been made.

On the verso are other studies of Venetian gothic.

The paper used for this sheet and for nos. 2277 and 2278 is the same, and although that is not proof of common authorship. I cannot follow Manteuffel in refusing this to Pisanello, on the alleged grounds of coarseness of technique, too generalized conception of the personality, etc. while he accepts the two others as authentic.

Gaz. des Beaux Arts, II, xxiv, 1881, p. 179; Vent., p. 89; Hill, p. 105; Mant., p. 146; *Dessins*, 75 (recto) and 166 (verso); Marle, pp. 110, 148.

PLATE VIII

N° 8. — Louvre, Vallardi, 2277, fol. 21 Pen on grayish paper (no watermark). 27.5 × 19.5 cm.

Various studies: A man's leg in figured stocking, seen from behind; a ring containing a pointed stone; a crown; a circular design containing a dog seated to left among flowers, his head reverted; in the upper part of the circle a " nebuly " ornamentation; a courtier in figured cloak, seen from behind, his head in right profile; the above-mentioned dog in the same attitude, muzzled and wearing ornamental harness; four notes of flowers.

Manteuffel by a slip says that this sheet contains among other things the arms of Alfonso of Aragon; he has confused it with no. 2278. The circular design suggests a medal (we are reminded of the *impresa* used on a later medal of Francesco Sforza, a dog seated under a tree); but the " nebuly " ornament seems unsuitable. Nevertheless since the same ornament decorates the top of a circular design on no. 2278 containing the arms of the Gonzaga, it is possible that the two designs are for a medal.

Gir., 12166; Vent., p. 90; Hill, p. 205; Mant., p. 118; *Dessins*, 281; Marle, p. 186.

PLATE IX

N° 9. — Louvre, Vallardi, 2278, fol. 22. Pen on grayish paper (water-mark, pig ?). 27.7 × 19.7 cm.

Various studies: (1) Virgin seated, holding the Child on her knee; on the left, two cherubs' heads. (2) Shield of arms : quarterly 1 and 4 a lion, 2 and 3 . . . bars. Supported by two putti and enclosed in a circle at the top of which is a " nebuly " ornament as on no. 2277. (3) Below, two figures of men in court dress and various studies of ornament.

The arms have inexcusably been described by myself and others as those of Alfonso of Aragon. There can be little doubt that, as Mr Van de Put observes, they are the old Gonzaga coat : quarterly : 1 and 4, *gu.* the Bohemian lion *arg.* crowned *or*; 2 and 3 *or* three bars *sable.* This coat, according to Litta, was in use from 1365 to 1433, when the Gonzaga received from the Emperor Sigismund the arms : *arg.* a cross *gu.* betwen four eagles displayed *sa.* But the old arms continued to be borne as an escutcheon of pretence, on the new shield. Thus it is not certain that this drawing must date from before 1433. Indeed, if the circular designs on it and on no. 2277 are for a medal, it is hardly to be dated before 1438, when Pisanello made the first medal of which we have any record. There is good reason for dating his medal of Gianfrancesco Gonzaga about 1439; at any rate he was in Mantua in May of that year.

Vent., p. 90; Mant., p. 118; *Dessins*, 77; Marle, p. 186.

PLATE X

N° 10. — Louvre, His de la Salle, 423 verso. Pen on paper, tinted red on recto, gray on verso. 24.3 × 18 cm.

Various studies; Sketch of the walls of a city, with Ghibelline battlements. Two studies in left profile of the bust of Niccolò III d'Este, in a large hat (as on no. 2276). Bust of Faustina the Elder to right under a Gothic arch; below, DIVA FAVSTINA PISANVS HOC OPVS; all in a rectangular panel.

The man is evidently the same as the one on no. 2276 (see Pl. VII) and therefore more probably Niccolo d'Este than Gianfrancesco Gonzaga. The profile of Faustina is doubtless, as the label DIVA FAVSTINA indicates, taken not from a bust but from a sestertius. Had it been done from a bust, it would more likely have been in three-quarter view or facing. The very incongruous gothic architectural setting suggests that this may have been one of a series of Imperial portraits forming the decoration of a room.

Manteuffel, though he places the sheet in limbo, thinks that this portion may perhaps be a copy after Pisanello. Though the label PISANVS HOC OPVS does not prove it to be his own work, it is at least not a certain disproof of his authorship.

On the recto, a monk holding a drinking-glass, and a kneeling figure.

Gir. no number. Both de Tauzia, *Not. des Dessins de la Coll. His de la Salle*, 1881, p. 58, no. 81; Vent., p. 121; Hill, p. 23 and in *Papers of the British School at Rome*, iii, 1906, p. 296; Mant., p. 176.

PLATE XI

Nº 11. — Louvre, Vallardi, 2482, fol. 87. Black chalk on white paper (water mark, dragon?). 30.8 × 20.8 cm.

Profile study of bust of Niccolò Piccinino to left. The cap is exactly as on the medal (Hill, pl. 33); but he wears civilian dress instead of armour; what is more, the nose seems slightly more curved in the drawing. There is reason to suppose that the medal was made about 1441, and the drawing may be presumed to date from the same time. I do not know what Manteuffel means by saying that the heads in the drawing and the medal are turned in opposite directions. He notices a certain weakness or softness ('Flauheit') which distinguishes this drawing from the group of silverpoints with which its technical execution connects it, and he has consequently some hesitation in accepting it as the master's own work. It is however hardly reasonable to speak of a chalk drawing and a silverpoint as carried out in the same technique and find fault with the former for a certain quality which is largely accounted for by the medium used.

Gir., 12252; *L'Art*, viiii, i, 1882, p. 231; Vent., p. 97; Hill, pl. 34; Mant., p. 128 *Dessins*, 246; Marle, p. 160.

PLATE XII

Nº 12. — Louvre, Vallardi, 2323, fol. 67. Brush on parchment. 14.5 × 11.6 cm.

Bust to right, with head three quarters right, of Giangaleazzo Visconti. There is no doubt about the identification of the person, and the authorship of Pisanello is generally admitted; but, as Giangaleazzo died in 1402, the artist was probably copying an older portrait, possibly a miniature in a manuscript. The pose shews that it is unlikely to have been copied from or designed for a medal. The 'nebuly' ornament marking the truncation of the bust is to be observed, and compared with that on Plates VIII, IX.

This drawing used to be numbered 2325. Gir., 12144; Alinari, 1621; Both de Tauzia, 2ᵉ *not.*, p. 54, nº 1991; Heiss, p. 43; Vent., p. 94; Hill, p. 191 n.; Mant., p. 121.

Nº 13. — Louvre, Vallardi, 2324, fol. 67. Brush on parchment. 7.8 × 5.5 cm.

Head of a young negro three-quarters left.

Vent., p. 94; Mant., p. 121; *Dessins*, 112; Marle, p. 170.

N° 14. — Louvre, Vallardi, 2321, fol. 66. Silverpoint and watercolour on parchment. 9.9×7.6 cm.

Very careful drawing of the head in right profile of a young man, wearing a coat with a fur collar, the face finished with slight touches of watercolour.

Gir., 12143; Braun, 191; Both de Tauzia, 2e *notice*, p. 54, n° 1990; Vent., p. 94; Mant., p. 120; [the head which I have suggested (*Pisanello*, p. 192 note), may be Borso d'Este is not, as Manteuffel supposes, this, but no 2322].

N° 15. — Louvre, Vallardi, 2314, fol. 63. Silverpoint on parchment. 13×8.9 cm.

Profile of head of young man to left, perhaps Borso d'Este. Another drawing (pen on parchment, Vallardi, 2322, fol. 66; *Dessins*, 111), certainly represents Borso, being exactly like the medal of him by Amadio da Milano. Paolo Giovio is authority for the existence of a medal of Borso by Pisanello. But he is a bad authority, and has probably made a confusion with Amadio's medal. Manteuffel, accepting the pen-drawing Vallardi 2322 as a portrait of Borso by Pisanello, constructs the theory that Pisanello really did a medal of Borso, and that Amadio's medals of Borso and Leonello are copies of Pisanello's : Amadio's Leonello reproduces the *impresa* of the lynx, which is the subject of Pisanello's medal of the same prince, and " proves itself, by the weakening of the original, to be a copy "; wherefore " the conclusion lies to hand that Amadio's Borso medal is also the imitation of one by Pisanello, and the drawing V. 2322 is a study for the latter. " This drawing V. 2322 appears to me on the contrary so weak that an ascription to Amadio himself, a timid and hesitating craftsman, seems much more probable.

Vent., p. 93; Mant., p. 119; *Dessins*, 202; Marle, 168.

PLATE XIII

N° 16. — British Museum, 1895 — 9 — 15 — 441. Pen and ink over black chalk on white paper. 19.5×28.5 cm.

Six studies of corpses hanging from gallows; three-quarter length of a lady to left, wearing wreath of flowers; and a bust of a boy facing.

The gallows-studies are two views each of three victims; of the four in the top row, the first and the third, counting from the right, were used for the fresco in S. Anastasia; but in the fresco they have changed places with each other. The second and fourth studies represent a third corpse in an advanced stage of decomposition — a horrible sight, which the master did not perpetuate in the fresco.

The two figures which were used for the fresco appear again on a sheet of drawings in Mr Henry Oppenheimer's collection (from the Marquess of Lansdowne's collection; Sotheby's Sale, 25 Mar. 1920 lot 15; *Burl. Mag.*, vol. XXXVI, 1920, pp. 152 and 306).

There are the two complete corpses, hanging in the same relative position as in the fresco; there are also detailed drawings of their bodies from the waist downwards on a slightly larger scale. In this larger study of the legs of the right-hand figure the arrangement of the hose has been modified in a way which is exactly reproduced in the fresco. This fact, and the fact that the two bodies are in the same position relatively to each other, shew that Mr. Oppenheimer's sheet was actually in the artist's hand at the time of the painting of the fresco, the one here reproduced being a preliminary study.

From the Lagoy and Malcolm Collections. Dodgson in Prussian *Jahrbuch*, XV, 1894, p. 259 (reversed in the plate). Hill, p. 94; Mant., p. 130; Hill, in *Burl. Mag.*, vol. xxxvi, 1920, p. 307; Marle, p. 141, fig. 84.

PLATE XIV

N° 17. — Louvre, Vallardi, 2343, fol. 93. Pen on reddened paper (no watermark). 24.3 × 18.3 cm.

Right profile of the head of the Princess of the S. Anastasia fresco, the hair dressed as in that fresco, where however she faces to the left. Manteuffel regards this as one of the drawings made for transfer to the fresco. The evidence which he gives as to the measurements in the drawing and the fresco is on the face of it not very convincing, and before any decision can be based on it the fresco should be measured again. For another study of the same lady's head, see no. 2342.

On the verso, the head in left profile of a muzzled dog with rich collar (its straps touched with gold) inscribed with a motto now illegible; this is the head of the greyhound in the same fresco; the drawing has been re-inked.

Gir., 12108; Vent., p. 97; Mant., pp. 65, 133; *Dessins*, 82; Marle, p. 132. The verso: Hill, pl. 22; *Dessins*, 41.

PLATE XV

N° 18. — Louvre, Vallardi, 2325, fol. 68. Silverpoint and pen (?) on parchment. 17.8 × 23 cm.

Studies of Orientals: half figure of a Kalmuck archer to front, holding bow and arrow; and four heads (of which one is a tonsured monk). The study of the Kalmuck was used for the fresco of S. Anastasia, where only his head and shoulders are seen.

This sheet is wrongly numbered 2323 in some earlier descriptions. Gir., 12147; Both de Tauzia, 2e *notice*, p. 55, n° 1993; Vent., p. 94; Hill, p. 92, pl. 20; Mant., p. 121; Marle, p. 132 and fig. 78.

PLATE XVI

Nº 19. — Chantilly, Musée Condé. Pen and watercolour (green, blue and red) on parchment. 27.3 × 19.5 cm.

A courtier wearing a hat with scarf depending from it, and a lady in sweeping robes, her hair dressed like that of the Princess in the S. Anastasia fresco. (On the verso, pen drawings of a seated monk, a youth holding a hawk, a standing figure wearing an imperial crown.)

The costume studies belong to the same group as two other studies on parchment, one at Bayonne and the other at Oxford. One of the men in the latter wears long sweeping robes which have caused him to be taken for a woman; the two figures in the Bayonne drawing are certainly men.

Formerly in the Lagoy Collection. Purchased by the Duc d'Aumale from Reiset. Exp. de l'École des Beaux-Arts, 1879; Braun nº 165 (recto), 165 bis (verso); Gir., 796 (new nº 7854); Müntz, *Hist.*, i at p. 312 (wrongly described as from Malcolm Coll.); Vent., p. 126; Hill, pl. 23; Mant., p. 130. The Bayonne drawing: pen and ink and watercolour on parchment 26.5 × 18 cm. On left, above, very faint, a head in profile to right. Marks of Esdaile (1820), Lagoy and L. Bonnat. Verso: pen and bistre; three male saints standing to front and studies of six birds. The recto reproduced by Vent., p. 125 and Van Marle, p. 71; phot. Braun and Les Archives des Arts. For the Oxford drawing see Colvin, *Drawings of the Old Masters in the University Galleries and in the Library of Christ Church*, Oxford, II, pl. 27.

PLATE XVII

Nº 20. — Louvre, Vallardi, 2468, fol. 277. Pen on white paper (no watermark). 20 × 16.5 cm.

Two horses, saddled and harnessed, one of them three-quarters to front, the other foreshortened from behind. The nostrils of one (those of the other are not visible) are slit. This form of mutilation evidently excited the curiosity of Pisanello, who, as the number of drawings of horses' muzzles by or after him indicates, was intensely interested in this part of the animal. On the much discussed drawing connected with the Emperor John Palaeologus (see above, p. 20), there is a horse's head similarly maltreated. It may therefore be conjectured that the practice was employed, if not by the Byzantines themselves, then by some Eastern race from which their stables were supplied. The same practice is illustrated in the S. Anastasia fresco (among the group of riders, the second horse from the left with lowered head).

On the practice, Mr Hinton of the Natural History Museum refers me to the following extract from Youatt, *The Horse*, London, 1868, p. 198 : " the inhabitants of some countries were accustomed to slit the nostrils of their horses that they might be less distressed in the severe and long-continued exertion of their speed. The Icelanders do so to the present day ". Further, Sir Alfred Pease writes : " I have seen it done in Africa, but not often, but in the Sahara in 1899 and 1900 I saw many donkeys with their noses slit. It is the common practice with the Mzabis in the Beni Mzab Confederated Cities which I visited in 1899-1900..... I asked the people at Guerara... why they did it — the answer always was 'they breathe more freely.' There were no horses in Guerara in those days or I suppose they would have had their nostrils slit. »

M. J. Buhot also calls my attention to the fact that quite recently Prof. A. von Lecoq found a similar custom prevailing amongst the Mongols in Turkestan. « Um Pferde bei Ueberanstrengungen, wenn sie nicht mehr weiter können, zu heilen, schneidet man ihnen ein Stück Knorpel aus der Nase. Ob dieses Verfahren irgendwelchen Nutzen bringt und auf Erfahrung beruht, vermag ich nicht zu sagen. » (A von Lecoq, *Auf Hellas Spuren in Ost-Turkistan*, Leipzig, 1926, p. 79, l. 11 sqq.).

Gir., 15115 (old n° 205); Vent., p. 118; *Dessins*, 50; Mant., p. 128.

PLATE XVIII

N° 21. — Louvre, Vallardi, 2444, fol. 231. Pen on white paper (no watermark). 19.2 × 11.8 cm.

A horse seen from behind, foreshortened three-quarters to left, his tail tied up. Bears a general resemblance to horses in the S. Anastasia fresco and on the medal of Novello Malatesta.

Gir., 12236 ; *Gaz. des Beaux-Arts*, III, xi, 1894, p. 425 f; Vent., p. 113 ; Hill, p. 95, pl. 24 ; Mant., p. 127 ; *Dessins*, 7 ; *L'Arte*, 1920, p. 9 ; Marle, p. 143, fig. 85.

PLATE XIX

N° 22. — Louvre, Vallardi, 2378, fol. 171. Pen on white paper (no watermark). 22.3 × 16.6 cm.

Saddled and harnessed horse, seen from behind, foreshortened three-quarters to right ; branded on the right hind haunch with a circle surmounted by a cross.

Sometimes regarded as a study for the medal of Novello Malatesta ; but, as Manteuffel observes, the position is different and the tail is not tied up. The brand, which resembles the ornament worn by a man on nº 2339, fol. 86, is perhaps meant to suggest the Imperial orb and cross; if so, the horse may have belonged to the stables of John VIII Palaeologus, and have been studied at Ferrara, in 1438.

Gir., 12204; H. de Chennevières, *Les Dessins du Louvre, Le Pisan,* pl. 2; Both de Tauzia, 2e *notice,* p. 57, nº 1999; Vent., p. 105; Hill, pp. 95, 166, note 3; Mant., p. 123.

PLATE XX

Nº 23. — Louvre, Vallardi, 2369, fol. 165. Pen over chalk on white paper (no watermark). 15.3 × 20.2 cm.

Horse lying on its side to left, the off legs drawn up.

Gir., 12206a; Vent., p. 104; Mant., p. 123; *Dessins,* 127.

PLATE XXI

Nº 24. — Louvre, Vallardi, 2370, fol. 165. Pen on white paper (watermark, moor's head). 15.7 × 24.1 cm.

Horse lying on its side to left, all the legs extended. This and the preceding are two independent studies of doubtless the same animal; one is not a copy of the other. Nor is it certain that the animal is dead, as some have supposed.

Gir., 12206b; Vent., p. 104; Mant., p. 123; *Dessins,* 145; Marle, p. 154, note 5.

PLATE XXII

Nº 25. — Louvre, Vallardi, 2455, fol. 267. Pen and brush, bistre and watercolour on parchment. 15.8 × 15.2 cm.

Forepart of a horse and two separate studies of the mouth and one of the eye. "Not by Pisanello" (Manteuffel).

Vent., p. 117; Mant., p. 158; *Dessins,* 117.

Nº 26. — Louvre, Vallardi, 2405, fol. 198. Pen and bistre on parchment. 11.7 × 10 cm.
The head of a horse with slit nostrils, pricking its ears, seen from the front. On the slit nostrils, see note on Pl. XVII.

Vent., p. 109; Mant., p. 125; *Dessins,* 116.

PLATE XXIII

N° 27. — Louvre, Vallardi, 2361, fol. 150. Pen on white paper (no watermark). 23.7 × 18.7 cm.

Head of a horse in left profile, richly harnessed and bridled, tassel falling over forehead. For the S. Anastasia fresco.

Vent., p. 102; Mant., p. 122; *Dessins*, 51.

PLATE XXIV

N° 28. — Louvre, Vallardi, 2363, fol. 152. Pen on white paper (watermark, moor's head). 27.8 × 18.7 cm.

Head of a haltered horse to right, turned slightly to front, with slit nostrils. On the slit nostrils, see note on pl. XVII.

Vent., p. 103; Mant., p. 123; *Dessins*, 55.

PLATE XXV

N° 29. — Louvre, Vallardi, 2360, fol. 149. Pen on white paper (no watermark). 26.9 × 16.8 cm.

Head of horse to front, with bridle hanging.

Vent., p. 102; Mant., p. 122; *Dessins*, 118.

PLANCHE XXVI

N° 30. — Louvre, Vallardi, 2358, fol. 147. Pen on white paper (watermark, moor's head). 22.5 × 17.9 cm.

Head of horse to right, with hanging bridle. Has no connexion with the horse on the medal of Lodovico Gonzaga, as it is said by Guiffrey-Venturi to have.

Vent., p. 102; Hill, p. 171, note; Mant., p. 122; *Dessins*, 52; J. Meder, Die *Handzeichnung*, 2d. ed. 1923, p. 452.

PLATE XXVII

N° 31. — Louvre, Vallardi, 2357, fol. 146. Pen on white paper (watermark, moor's head). 23.4 × 18.3 cm.

Head of horse to right, bridled. Has a merely general resemblance to one in the fresco of S. Anastasia.

Vent., p. 102; Mant., p. 122; *Dessins*, 151.

PLATE XXVIII

N° 32. — Louvre, Vallardi, 2356, fol. 145. Pen, touched with watercolour, on white paper (no watermark,). 26 × 19.7 cm.

Head of bridled horse in profile to right, and a foreleg. The close connexion with the St Eustace of this beautiful drawing is generally admitted. Manteuffel, who has persuaded himself that the picture is the work of an imitator, rejects the drawing also. His argument is significant; — " this study, or the picture for which it was intended, was used by an imitator in the St Eustace of the National Gallery... It might be by Pisano, if the closely connected drawing no. 2366 did not make that very improbable. " No. 2366, a study of the hind quarters and legs of a horse, is also closely connected with the same picture.

Vent., p. 102; Mant., p. 152; *Dessins*, 155.

PLATE XXIX

N° 33. — Louvre, Vallardi, 2355, fol. 144. Pen on white paper (no watermark). 23.5 × 16 cm.

Head of a bridled horse in left profile. Connected — in the usual degree — with the fresco in S. Anastasia and the *St George and St Anthony* of the National Gallery.

Vent., p. 101; Mant., p. 122; *Dessins*, 119.

PLATE XXX

N° 34. — Louvre, Vallardi, 2354, fol. 143. Pen on white paper (no watermark). 29.1 × 18.5 cm.

Two studies of a horse's head, with bit in mouth, and a third of the nose. General studies, without special reference, so far as we know, to any particular picture.

Gir., 12199; Vent., p. 102; Mant., p. 122; *Dessins*, 173.

PLATE XXXI

N° 35. — Louvre, Vallardi, 2353, fol. 142. Pen on white paper (watermark, moor's head). 25.2 × 19.1 cm.

Four studies of horses' muzzles, with slit nostrils. On this last feature, see note on Pl. XVII.

Vent., p. 102; Mant., p. 122; *Dessins*, 53.

PLATE XXXII

N° 36. — Louvre, Vallardi, 2352, fol. 141. Pen on white paper (watermark, moor's head). 17.2 × 23.8 cm.

Three studies of a horse's mouth and nose and a slight sketch of a horse's chest. These were used for the fresco in S. Anastasia, perhaps also for the London *St George and St Anthony*.

Vent., p. 102; Mant., p. 121; *Dessins*, 154.

PLATE XXXIII

N° 37. — Louvre, Vallardi, 2380, fol. 174. Pen on white paper (no watermark). 18.8 × 25 cm.

Mule, saddled, harnessed and bitted, standing to left. A study which was evidently used for the fresco ot S. Anastasia.

Gir., 12203; Chennevières, *Les Dessins du Louvre, le Pisan*, pl. II; *L'Art*, VIII, i, 1882, p. 229; Both de Tauzia, *Deuxième notice*, p. 57, n° 1998; Müntz, *Hist.*, I, p. 639; Vent., pp. 105-6; Mant., p. 123; Marle, p. 148 note 1 and fig. 88.

PLATE XXXIV

N° 38. — Louvre, Vallardi, 2458, fol. 270. Chalk on parchment. 15.2 × 18.8 cm.
An ass standing to left, its ears laid back.

Vent., p. 117; Mant., p. 127; *Dessins*, 121.

N° 39. — Louvre, Vallardi, 2493, fol. 237. Pen on white paper (no watermark). 9.8 × 14 cm.

A captive chamois lying to right, its forelegs tied together.

Gir., 12219; Vent., p. 114; Mant., p. 129; *Dessins*, 220.

PLATE XXXV

N° 40. — Louvre, Vallardi, 2489, fol. 234. Pen on white paper (watermark, moor's head). 20.2 × 27.7 cm.

A stag seen from behind, lying down to left, head turned away.

Gir., 12217; Vent., p. 113; Mant., p. 129; *Dessins*, 172.

PLATE XXXVI

N° 41. — Louvre, Vallardi, 2490, fol. 235. Pen on white paper (no watermark). 15.8 × 20.8 cm.

Two studies of the head of a stag, and the head of a doe. One of the former is fairly near the stag bearing a Crucifix in the *St Eustace*; Manteuffel, since he accepts this drawing as Pisanello's, denies any such connexion.

Gir., 12218; Vent., p. 113; Mant., p. 129; *Dessins*, 233.

PLATE XXXVII

N° 42. — Louvre, Vallardi, 2492, fol. 236. Silverpoint and watercolour on parchment. 20.2 × 25.3 cm.

A stag standing to left, only the head finished in bistre and watercolour. To the right, above its crupper, another light sketch of the same beast. The connexion with the Crucifix-bearing stag in the *St Eustace* is close, but not necessarily closer than it would be in the case of any two studies of such animals seen in left profile. Manteuffel is quick to point this out. The chief, perhaps the only, variation is in the antlers; in this respect the head on the left in no. 2490 (Pl. XXXVI) is much closer to the picture.

Gir., 12217; Vent., p. 113; Hill, p. 69 note, Pl. 13; Mant., p. 143; *Dessins,* 85; Marle, p. 80.

PLATE XXXVIII

N° 43. — Louvre, Vallardi, 2494, fol. 237. Pen on parchment. 12.8 × 18.9 cm.

Two studies of a stag (fallow-deer), one of its head, and two guinea-fowls (*Numida meleagris*).

Gir., 12219; Vent., p. 114; Mant., p. 129; *Dessins,* 86 and 247; Marle, p. 81, fig. 44.

N° 44. — Louvre, Vallardi, 2497, fol. 242. Brush and watercolour on parchment. 11.1 × 13.9 cm.

Young roebuck (*capreolus capreolus*) standing to right, the horns still in the velvet.

Gir., 12163; Both de Tauzia, *Deuxième notice,* p. 58, no. 2002; Vent., p. 114; Mant., p. 143; *Dessins,* 262.

PLATE XXXIX

N° 45. — Louvre, Vallardi, 2433, fol. 223. Pen and watercolour on white paper (no watermark). 18.4 × 24.5 cm.

Greyhound standing to right.

Gir., 12229; Vent., p. 111; Mant., pp. 72, 157; *Dessins,* 79.

PLATE XL

N° 46. — Louvre, Vallardi, 2434, fol. 224. Pen on white paper (no watermark). 16 × 19.5 cm.

A greyhound, prick-eared, muzzled and collared, standing to left. This study was used for the hound in the fresco of S. Anastasia.

Gir., 12228; *Gaz. des Beaux Arts,* III, xi, 1894, p. 421; Vent., p. 112; Hill, p. 95 pl. 25; Mant., p. 127; *Dessins,* 6; *L'Arte,* 1920, p. 8.

PLATE XLI

N° 47. — Louvre, Vallardi, 2435, fol. 225. Pen and watercolour on white paper (no watermark). 16.5 × 25 cm.

A greyhound standing to left, wearing red muzzle and a red collar studded with silver nails. According to Manteuffel, not even of the fifteenth century.

Gir., 12263; *L'Art,* VIII, i, 1882, p. 225 ; Both de Tauzia, 2e *Notice,* 1888, p. 57, no. 2000; Müntz, *Hist.,* I, 1889, 37. *Arch. Stor. dell'Arte,* III, 1890, p. 148; Vent., p. 111; Mant., p. 157; Marle, p. 147, fig. 89.

PLATE XLII

N° 48. — Louvre, Vallardi, 2430, fol. 221. Pen and watercolour on white paper (no watermark). 16 × 23.9 cm.

Head of a greyhound to right.

Gir., 12229; Vent., p. 111; Mant., pp. 72, 157; *Dessins,* 208.

PLATE XLIII

N° 49. — Louvre, Vallardi, 2429, fol. 220. Black chalk (very faint) and watercolour on white paper (no watermark). 18.3 × 21.9 cm.

Head of a hound (pointer or "bracco") to right; the eye, nose and corner of mouth touched with watercolour. One of the most delicate drawings in the whole series, and the watercolour very skilfully and sensitively applied (but in a manner, if we are to believe Manteuffel, foreign to Pisanello and indeed to the Quattrocento).

On the verso, study in black chalk of the hound with reverted head in the *St Eustace* "Perhaps an original drawing by the Master of the St Eustace." (Mant.)

Vent., p. 111; W. Arkwright, *The Pointer and his Predecessors*. frontisp. and p. 203; Mant., pp. 72, 157; *Dessins*, 176.

PLATE XLIV

N° 50. — Louvre, Vallardi, 2423, fol. 215. Pen and watercolour on white paper (no watermark). 13.7 × 21,4 cm.

A fox lying to left.

Gir., 12209; Vent., p. 111; Mant., p. 140; *Dessins*, 267.

PLATE XL

N° 51. — Louvre, Vallardi, 2424, fol 215. Watercolour on parchment. 16.2 × 22.5 cm.

A wolf standing to left.

Gir., 12209; Vent., p. 111; Mant., p. 140; *Dessins*, 188. Marle, p. 89, fig. 50.

PLATE XLVI

N° 52. — Louvre, Vallardi, 2419, fol. 212. Pen over chalk on reddened paper (no watermark). 24.8 × 18.3 cm.

Head and forebody of a wolf or wild dog to left. On the verso, studies of flowers (see Pl. LXI).

No. 2418, fol. 211 (Gir., 12208, *Dessins*, 132), in pen and ink over chalk. on reddened paper, also has two studies of the head and forebody of a similar animal, and very faint traces of the body of another in chalk. The animal has always hitherto been taken for a wild cat, but I am assured by my colleagues at the Natural History Museum that it is not so.

Gir., 12239 (recto); Vent., p. 110; Mant., p. 126; *Dessins*, 131 (recto).

PLATE XLVII

N° 53. — Louvre, Vallardi, 2425, fol. 216. Pen and bistre and watercolour on parchment. 16.3 × 14. 3 cm.

Study of a cheetah or hunting-leopard springing to left, wearing a collar; also three twisted columns. The cheetah is finished in watercolour.

Vent., p. 111; Mant., p. 140 (confuses this with no. 2426); *Dessins*, 271.

PLATE XLVIII

N° 54. — Louvre, Vallardi, 2426, fol. 216. Pen and watercolour on parchment. 16 × 23.1 cm.

A cheetah or hunting-leopard springing to right; wears a red collar.

Gir., 12207; Vent., p. 111; Mant., p. 140 (confuses this with no. 2425); *Dessins*, 178; Marle, p. 75.

PLATE XLIX

N° 55. — Louvre, Vallardi, 2422, fol. 214. Silverpoint on parchment. 15 × 23.3 cm.

A cat lying to left. It is probably a domestic cat, the tail being rather long for the wild cat.

Gir., 12240; Vent., p. 111; Mant., p. 127; *Dessins*, 133.

PLATE L

N° 56. — Louvre, Vallardi, 2409, fol. 202. Silverpoint and brush on parchment. 14.5 × 20.5 cm.

A pair of buffaloes, yoked and belled, walking to left.

Gir., 12223; Vent., p. 110; Mant., p. 125; *Dessins*, 46.

PLATE LI

N° 57. — Louvre, Vallardi, 2410, fol. 203. Silverpoint (touched with brush ?) on parchment. 17 × 23.1 cm.

Cow lying down to left, about to get up. This has no relation, as Gruyer supposed, to the Berlin tondo; the cow in that picture is not about to rise.

Gir., 12220; *Gaz. des Beaux Arts,* III, xii, 1894, p. 489; Vent., p. 110; Mant., p. 125; *Dessins,* 45; *L'Arte,* 1920, p. 127; Marle, p. 174, fig. 104.

PLATE LII

N° 58. — Louvre, Vallardi, 2411, fol. 204. Silverpoint and pen, touched with the brush, on parchment. 17.6 × 22.6 cm.

Three studies of oxen lying down.

Gir., 12221; Vent., p. 110; Mant., p. 126; *Dessins,* 195.

PLATE LIII

N° 59. — Louvre, Vallardi, 4217, fol. 210. Pen and watercolour on white paper (no watermark). 14 × 20 cm.

A boar standing to right.

In the Collection of Sir Edward Poynter (Sale, 1918; Vasari Society, V, 4; Van Marle, p. 185, fig. 114) was an uncoloured drawing of a boar to left, in some ways finer than this.

Gir., 12262; *L'Art,* VIII, i, 1882, p. 224; Both de Tauzia, 2e *Notice,* 1888, p. 57, no. 2001; Müntz, *Hist.,* I, 1889, p. 343; Vent., p. 110; Mant., p. 140.

PLATE LIV

N° 60. — Louvre, Vallardi, 2485, fol. 258. Pen over chalk on parchment. 23.5 × 17.1 cm.

Two studies of heraldic eagles displayed and crowned.

On the verso, very faint sketch of a saddled ass. These eagles are of course for some heraldic design; possibly the Gonzaga arms, since they are crowned, rather than for the Este coat, in which they are usually uncrowned.

On the verso of a sheet in the British Museum are pen studies of eagles so closely resembling these " that one drawing would seem to have been produced by transfer from the other, were it not that the dimensions of the birds have been altered " (Hill, p. 239). I think the British Museum drawing may be a copy of the one here reproduced.

Gir., 12178; *Gaz. des Beaux Arts,* II, XXIV, 1881, p. 79 note; *L'Art,* VIII, I, 1882, p. 228; Both de Tauzia, *Deuxième notice,* 1888, p. 56, no. 1997; Müntz, *Hist.,* I, 1889, p. 644; Vent., p. 115; Hill, p. 201, note; Mant., p. 128.

PLATE LV

N° 61. — Louvre, Vallardi, 2452, fol. 265. Pen on parchment. 24.2 × 15.7 cm.

A hooded falcon (*Falco peregrinus peregrinoides,* or " Banbury falcon ") seen from behind. The hood is very lightly indicated in silverpoint. On the verso, four falcons and a mouse, in bistre, with fine brush.

Vent., p. 117; Mant., p. 141; *Dessins,* 159 recto, 257 verso.

PLATE LVI

N° 62. — Louvre, Vallardi, 2453, fol. 265. Pen and watercolour on white paper (watermark, moor's head). 23.7 × 15 cm.

Falcon, with blue hood, seen from behind, perched on falconer's wrist. Corresponds in pose exactly to the uncoloured drawing no. 2452 (Pl. LV) and is the same bird; but the other drawing does not shew the falconer's hand.

Gir., 15114; Vent., p. 117; Mant., p. 141; *Dessins,* 196.

FRONTISPIECE

N° 63. — Louvre, Vallardi, 2472, fol. 281. Pen and watercolour on parchment. 18.3 × 27.1 cm.

Fourteen egrets.

Compare the drawing no. 2471 fol. 280, on which, however, one of the birds has been coloured by an unskilled hand (*Dessins*, 61). These drawings have the same general relation to the *St Eustace* as no. 2450 (Pl. LVII).

Gir., 12196; *Gaz. des Beaux-Arts*, III, XII, 1894, p. 297; Vent., p. 119; Mant., p. 142; *Dessins*, 279.

PLATE LVII

N° 64. — Louvre, Vallardi, 2450, fol. 263. Pen on white paper (no watermark). 24.5 × 17.5 cm.

An egret to right. One of many bird studies, such as must have been made for the *St Eustace*, though it does not correspond exactly with any one in that picture.

Gir., 12194; Vent., p. 117; Mant., p. 141; *Dessins*, 226.

PLATE LVIII

N° 65. — Louvre, Vallardi, 2467, fol. 276. Pen and watercolour over chalk on white paper (watermark, moor's head). 16.2 × 21.7 cm.

Two hoopoes, one finished in watercolour, finely. There may be a connexion with the bird in the *St Eustace*, below, on the right; that, however, seems to have been retouched

Gir., 12189; Vent., p. 118; Mant., p. 142; *Dessins*, 277.

PLATE LIX

N° 66. — Louvre, Vallardi, 2382, fol. 179. Silverpoint on parchment. 12 × 15.2 cm.

Lizard seen from above, spitted through the mouth; therefore a study for a dragon transfixed by the spear of St George.

Vent., p. 107; Mant., p. 124; *Dessins*, 270.

PLATE LX

N° 67. — Louvre, Vallardi, 2383, fol. 179. Silverpoint on parchment. 13.8 × 22.1 cm.

A lizard.

Vent., p. 107; Mant., p. 124; *Dessins*, 245.

PLATE LXI

N° 68. — Louvre, Vallardi, 2419, fol. 212 verso (See no. 52, Pl. XLVI). Pen over chalk on reddened paper (no watermark). 24.8 × 18.3 cm.

Studies of flowers. Beginning above, first row, from the left : (a) unidentified; (b) *Bellis* (? *B. perennis*, L.); (c) *Arum* (probably *Arum italicum*, L.). Second row, (d) ? *Pinguicola*; (e) and (f) a liliaceous bulb (? *Colchicum*). Third row, (g) ? *Crepis* or allied genus (*Compositae*) (h) same as (d). These identifications I owe to the Botanical Department of the Natural History Museum.

For the recto, see pl. XLVIII. Compare the sheet at Bayonne, from the Bonnat Coll., 00648 verso; pen and ink on parchment 26.2 × 18.5 cm.; studies of irises etc. (Vent., p. 124; Mant., p. 179.)

Vent., p. 110; Mant., p. 126; *Dessins*, 66.

PLATE LXII

N° 69. — Louvre, Vallardi, 2486, fol. 249. Pen on white paper (no watermark). 16.8 × 14.5 cm.

Study for a medal of Alfonso of Aragon (therefore of 1448 or 1449). The King riding an ambling horse to right, in armour, wearing a broad-brimmed hat. The horse is richly caparisoned. On its head, the royal crest of Aragon, or drac-pennat, a sort ot wyvern; on its crupper, a putto holding the shield of Aragon. Above, the royal crown between two shields : Aragon and Sicily on the right (sinister); Aragon, Naples, Jerusalem, etc. on the left (dexter). Below, the signature PISANI PICTORIS OPVS.

This medal was apparently never executed.

Gir., 12163; *Gaz. des Beaux Arts*, II, XXIV, 1881, p. 169; Heiss, p. 35; Both de Tauzia, *Deuxième notice*, 1888, p. 52, no. 1989; Vent., p. 115; Hill, p. 204, pl. 62; Mant., p. 128.

PLATE LXIII

N° 70. — Louvre, Vallardi, 2307, fol. 61. Pen on white paper (no watermark). 16.9 × 14.3 cm.

Study for the ‘ Liberalitas ’ medal of King Alfonso of Aragon. The King's bust to left, bare-headed, in mail, with a shoulder-piece adorned with a triple infant-face and bat's-wing edge; behind, his helmet, bearing the arms of Aragon supported on the sinister side (which alone is seen) by a griffin, and crested with a bat (the rat-pennat, being the royal crest adopted by James the Conquistador); above, DIVVS· | ALPHONSVS· | REX· in two lines; below, TRIVMPHATOR· | ET· | PACIFICVS in two lines; in front, the crown, below which, ·M· | ·CCCC· | ·XLVIII· | ·III· in four lines, the last two being lightly erased. (The first idea was doubtless to have the whole date in three lines, the second was to put the three units in a fourth line). The background is heavily shaded along parts of the contours to throw them into relief.

The medal, as actually completed, was considerably altered, but there is no doubt that this drawing was preliminary to the medal, and not merely a casual study. In the first place, the whole composition was made to face to the right. (It is indeed possible that the artist sometimes worked *in cavo*, cutting a mould in some material like plaster from which wax impressions would be taken; hence the bust in the completed model would look the other way). The King wears armour of plate over his shirt of mail; the somewhat grotesque shoulder-piece with its bat's-wing edging disappears,and for the bat-crest of the helmet is substituted a plain crest; the shield and supporter are removed from the helmet, which now bears on its side an open book seen from behind (known to be an *impresa* of Alfonso, and also used later by Ferdinand I). The crown is much simplified, and the date is placed partly above, partly below it, being altered to MCCCCXLVIIII. The date on the drawing shews that Pisanello, who was still in the North of Italy in August 1448, arrived in Naples before the end of that year; it was not however until February 14, 1449, that he was granted a regular salary by the King.

Gir., 12148; *Gaz. des Beaux Arts*, II, XXIV, 1881 p. 171; III, x, 1893, p. 357; Heiss, p. 33; Vent., p. 92; Hill, front. and p. 199; Mant., p. 118; *Dessins*, 38; J. Meder, *die Handzeichnung*, 2d. ed., 1923, p. 370.

PLATE LXIV

N° 71. — Louvre, Vallardi, 2306, fol. 61. Pen on white paper (no watermark). 20.7 × 14.8 cm.

Two drawings for the 'Venator intrepidus' medal of Alfonso of Aragon. Above, in a circle, the bust of the King to right, with his crown below it, and in two lines across: DIVVS· ALPHONSVS· REX | MCCCC XLVIII· Below, the King's bust alone repeated.

A much less finished sketch than that for the 'Liberalitas' medal (Pl. LXIII). In the medal (Hill, pl. 60), the inscription has been placed in a circle around the field instead of across it. The finished medal bears no date. On the verso, studies for textile ornament by another hand.

Gir., 12148; Vent., p. 92; Mant., p. 118; *Dessins*, 35.

CONCORDANCE

The first column contains the *numéro d'ordre* by which the drawings are arranged in the Cabinet des Dessins in the Louvre. The second, the old folio-number of the so-called Codex Vallardi. The third, the number of Giraudon's photograph, where such exists. (The numbers of M. Giraudon's old Catalogue of 1899 have all now been increased by 12000). In the fourth column appears the page of Guiffrey's Catalogue in Venturi's edition of Vasari's *Life*. In the fifth, the page of Kurt Zoege von Manteuffel's dissertation. In the sixth, the number of the plate in the *Dessins de Pisanello et de son École*, published by the Société de Reproduction des Dessins de Maîtres. In the seventh, the number of the reproduction (not the number of the Plate) in the present work. When a *numéro d'ordre* is omitted from this concordance, it means that the drawing concerned, even though it may be by Pisanello, is not to be found in any of the above-mentioned publications. The His de la Salle drawings are not included.

N°	FOLIO	GIR.	VENT.	MANT.	DESSINS	HILL.
2262	8	12170	89	145	70	
2263	9		89	145	69	
2264	10	12171	89	145	76	
2266	12		89	145	144	
verso					113	
2269	15		89	117		
2270	15		89	117		
2273				146		
2274						(p. 20)
2275	19		89	117	4	
verso					68	
2276	20		89	146	75	7
verso					166	(p. 31)

N°	FOLIO	GIR.	VENT.	MANT.	DESSINS	HILL.
2277	21	12166	90	118	281	8
2278	22		90	118	77	9
2280	37		90	146	234	(p. 18)
2281	38		90	147	222	
verso					192	
2287	43		90	147		
2288	44		90	147		
2289	45	12176	90	147	237	
2290	46		90	147	244	
2291	47	12245	91	147	33	
2292	48		91	147	250	
verso					219	
2293	49		91	148		
2294	50	12175	91	148	235	
2295	51		91	148	109	(p. 16)
verso					236	
2299	55	12142	92	148	30	
2300	58		92	148	74	
2301	59		92	118		
2303	59		92	149		
2305	60		92	149		
2306	61	12148	92	118	35	71
verso					36	
2307	61	12148	92	118	38	70
2308	62		93	118		
2309	62		93	119		
2310	62		93	119	203	
2311	63		93	119	199	
2313	63		93	119	110	
2314	63		93	119	202	
2315	64		93	132	209	
verso					103	
2316 (now 2320)	64	12143	93	149		
2317	65	12164	93	119		
2318	65	12164	94	120		
2319	65		94	149	266	
2320 see 2316						
2321	66	12143	94	120		14
2322	66		94	120	111	15 note
2323	67	12144	94	121		12
2324	67		94	121	112	13
2325	68	12147	94	121		18
2326	69		95	121		
2327	70		95	149		

N°	FOLIO	GIR.	VENT.	MANT.	DESSINS	HILL.
2328	71		95	150	223	(p. 19)
2329	72		95	150	102	(p. 19)
2330	73		95	150	104	
2331	74		95	150		
2332	75	12151	95	151	105	
verso		12150			106	
2333	76		96	151	204	
2334	77		96	151	240	
2335	78		96	151	242	(p. 19)
2336	79		96	151	107	(p. 19)
2337	82		96	151	224	(p. 19)
2338	84		96	151	24	(p. 19)
verso					22	
2339	86		97	152	31	(p. 20)
2342	92	12109	97	132	5	(p. 33)
verso		12111			81	
2343	93	12108	97	133	82	17
verso					41	
2344		12106				(p. 19)
2352	141		102	121	154	36
2353	142		102	122	53	35
2354	143	12199	102	122	173	34
2355	144		102	122	119	33
2356	145		102	152	155	32
2357	146		102	122	151	31
2358	147		102	122	52	30
2359	148		102	122	152	
2360	149		102	122	118	29
2361	150		102	122	51	27
2362	151		102	122	214	
2363	152		103	123	55	28
2364	159		103	152	123	
2365	160		104	152	190	
2366	161		104	152	122	32 note
2367	162		104	153	120	
2368	163		104	153	10	
verso					8	
2369	165	12206	104	123	127	23
2370	165	12206	104	123	145	24
2371	166		104	153	260	
2372	166		104	153	100	
2373	166		104	123	158	
2374	168		105	153	115	
2375	169		105	158	168	
2378	171	12204	105	123		22

Nº	FOLIO	GIR.	VENT.	MANT.	DESSINS	HILL.
2379	172		106	123	54	
2380	174	12203	106	123		37
2381	178		106	124	134	
2382	179		107	124	270	66
2383	179		107	124	245	67
2384					263	
2385	181	12241	107	124	197	
2387	183	12225	107	153	198	(p. 19)
2388	186	28716	107	154	169	
2389	187		107	154	150	
verso		28719				
2390	188	12210	107	154	174	
verso					153	
2391	189	12212	108	154		(p. 20)
verso					193	
2392	190	12144	108	154	80	
verso		28717			44	
2393	190	28718	108	154	231	
2394	191	12211	108	155	48	
2395	192	12213	108	155	125	
2396	193		108	124	42	
verso					43	
2397	194	12224	108	155	126	(p. 25)
verso		12168			20	1
2398	195	12156	109	124	18	6
2399	196	12226	109	125	129	
2400	196		109	125	130 et 251	
2403	198		109	156		
2405	198		109	125	116	26
2407	199		109	156	124	
2408	202		109	156	264	
2409	202	12223	110	125	46	56
2410	203	12220	110	125	45	57
2411	204	12221	110	126	195	58
2412	205		110	126	269	
2413	206		110	126	160	
2414	207		110	156	213	
2417	210	12262	110	140		59
2418	211	12208	110	126	132	52 note
2419	212	12239	110	126	131	52
verso					66	68
2420	213		111	127	205	
2421	214	12240	111	127	228	
2422	214	12240	111	127	133	55
2423	215	12209	111	140	267	50

N°	FOLIO	GIR.	VENT.	MANT.	DESSINS	HILL.
2424	215	12209	111	140	188	51
2425	216		111	140	271	53
2426	216	12207	111	140	178	54
2427	218		111	156	217	
2428	218		111	156	252	
2429	220		111	157	176	49
2430	221	12229	111	157	208	48
2431	222		111	157	268	
2432	219	12230	111	133	67	5
verso		12227			40	(p. 28)
2433	223	12229	111	157	79	45
2434	224	12228	111	127	6	46
2435	225	12263	111	157		47
2436	226		111	127	108	
2437	227		111	157	253	
2438	227	12235	111	157	175	
2439	227	12235	111	127	189	
2444	231	12236	113	127	7	21
2445	232	12234	113	158	84	
2446	232	12234	113	158	272	
2447	233	12242	113	158	212	
2448	261	12237	116	141	177	
verso					248	
2449	262		116	158	249	
2450	263	12194	117	141	226	64
2451	264	12238	117	158	136	
2452	265		117	141	159	61
verso					257	
2453	265	15114	117	141	196	62
2454	266	12182	117	141	143	
2455	267		117	158	117	25
2456	268		117	141	137	
2457	269	12181	117	158	157	
2458	270		117	127	121	38
2459	272	12184	117	141	280	
2460	272	12184	118	141	221	
2461	273	12183	118	142	239	
2462	273	12183	118	142		
2463	274	12185	118	142	138	
2464	275	12186	118	142	63	
2465	275	12186	118	142		
2466	276	12189	118	142	278	
2467	276	12189	118	142	277	65
2468	277	15115	118	128	50	20
2469	278		118	128	181	

Nº	FOLIO	GIR.	VENT.	MANT.	DESSINS	HILL.
2470	279		119	159	287	(p. 20)
2471	280	12198	119	142	61	63 note
2472	281	12196	119	142	279	63
2473	282	12190	119	142	56	
2474	283	12187	119	143	286	
2475	284	12188	119	143	59 et 285	
2476	284	12188	119	143		
2477	284	12188	119	143		
2478	80		96	159		(p. 23)
2479	81		96	159		
2480	83		96	159	191	
2481	85		96	159	9	
verso					58	
2482	87	12252	97	128	246	11
2483	88		97	160	32	(p. 23)
2484	89	12251	97	160	206	(p. 23)
2485	258	12178	115	128		60
2486	249	12163	115	128		69
2487	167		104	160	180	
2488	235		113	160	187	
2489	234	12217	113	129	172	40
2490	235	12218	113	129	233	41
2492	236	12217	113	143	85	42
2493	237	12219	114	129	220	39
2494	237	12219	114	129	86 et 247	43
2495	239	12214	114	160	128	
2496	240	12215	114	161	47	
verso					28	
2497	242	12163	114	143	262	44
2498	243	12231	114	161	148	
2500	247		115	129	161	
2501	247		114	143	210	
2502	247		114	129	265	
2503	248		115	161	207	
2504	248		115	161	135	
2505	248		115	161	254	
2506	250		115	161	238	
2507	251		115	161	62	
verso					64	
2508	252		115	161	60	
verso		12125			93	
2509	253	12192	115	162	141	
verso					23	
2510	254		115	162	139	
2511	255	12193	115	162	65	

N°	FOLIO	GIR.	VENT.	MANT.	DESSINS	HILL.
verso					57	
2512	256		115	162	149	
verso					225	
2513	257		115	129	229	
2514	259	12197	116	162	142	
2515	260	12191	116	162	156	
verso					241	
2520	5		88	163	16	
2521	4		88	163		
2522	5		88	163		
2523	6		88	163		
2533					282	
2534					258	
2537		12246				
2538	52		91	163	37	
2539	53	12177	91	163	283	
2540	54		92	164	284	
2541	175	12153	106	164	17	
verso		12155			1	
2542	176	12157	106	164	15	
verso		12158			101	
2544					243	
2545	200		109	164	227	
2546	201	12222	109	164	147	
2547	228	12232	113	164	184	
2549	241	12216	114	143	83	
2550	242		114	143	194	
2568	229	12233	113	165	211	
2589	94	12138	97	134	88	
verso		12110			182	(p. 26)
2591	97	12107	97	165	39	
2592	98		98	165	34	
2593	99	12123	98	165	179	
verso					78	
2594	100		98	134	29	(p. 27)
verso					21	(p. 17)
2595	101		98	134	13	(p. 27)
verso		12160			19	4
2596	102	12135	98	134	97	
verso		12172			261	
2597	103	12126	98	135	255	
verso		12249			256	
2598	104		98	135		
2599	105		98	135	186	
2600	106	12134	99	135	232	

N°	FOLIO	GIR.	VENT.	MANT.	DESSINS	HILL.
verso					215	
2601	107		99	135	146	
verso					14	
2602	108	12141	99	135	165	
verso		12124			89	
2603	109		99	135		
2604	110	12131	99	135	164	
verso					259	
2605	112	12140	99	136		
2606	113	12130	99	136	275	
verso		12254			94	
2607	114	12250	99	136	95	
verso		12139			90	
2608	115	12128	99	136	288	
2609	116	12127	100	136	27 et 218	
verso		12248			11	
2610	117	12118	100	136	163	
verso					201	
2611	118		100	136	92	
2612	119	12116	100	137	96	
2613	120	12115	100	137	12	
2614	121	12121	100	137	87	
2615	122	12120	100	137	230	
2616	123		100	137	185	
verso					183	
2617	124	12119	101	137	91	
2618	125	12132	101	137		
verso		12129			26	
2619	126	12122	101	138	276	
2620	127	12117	101	138	162	
2621	128	12113	101	138	25	
2622	129	12114	101	138	98	
2623	130	12133	101	166	170	
verso		12162			73	
2625	136	12243	101	166	216	
2626	137	12167	101	166	114	
2627	153		103	138	171	
2628	154		103	138	167	
2629	155		103	138		
2630	156		103	138	274	
2631	157		103	138		(p. 26)
verso		12165			273	3
2632	158	12201	103	139	49	
2633	173	12152	106	166	2	
verso		12159			3	

N°	FOLIO	GIR.	VENT.	MANT.	DESSINS	HILL.
2634	177	12161	106	167	99	
verso		12154			200	
2642		12145				
2643		12145				
2646		12146				
2647		12146				
2650	271	12180	117	144	140	
10707	184		107	167		
10708	185	12247	107	167		
M.I. 1062		13498		176	72	(p. 20)
verso					71	

INDEX

[*Louvre, Vallardi 2397, fol. 194 v.*]

PLATE I, No. 1. Nude figures from the antique.

[*British Museum, P.p. 11 v.*]

PLATE II, No. 2. Two allegorical figures.

PLATE III, No. 3. Various sketches, including a Virgin enthroned among four Saints. [*Louvre, Vallardi 2631, fol. 157 v.*]

[*Louvre, Vallardi 2595, fol. 101 v.*]

PLATE IV, No. 4. A party riding out into the country.

[*Louvre, Vallardi 2432, fol. 219.*]

PLATE V, No. 5. Studies of dogs, and of an audience in a hall.

[*Louvre, Vallardi 2398, fol. 195.*]

PLATE VI, No. 6. Two devils, an eagle, and other studies.

PLATE VII, No. 7. Studies of Venetian Gothic architecture; profile to left of Niccolò III d'Este.

[*Louvre, Vallardi 2276, fol. 20.*]

[*Louvre, Vallardi 2277, fol. 21.*]

PLATE VIII, No. 8. A dog seated to left among flowers, his head reverted; and other studies.

[*Louvre, Vallardi 2278, fol. 22.*]

PLATE IX, No. 9. Various studies, including a Virgin seated, and the arms of Gonzaga.

[*Louvre, His de la Salle, 423 v.*]

PLATE X, No. 10. Battlemented walls; two sketches in left profile of Niccolò III d'Este; "Diva Faustina."

[*Louvre, Vallardi 2482, fol. 87*]

PLATE XI, No. 11. Large profile of bust of Niccolò Piccinino to left.

[*Louvre, Vallardi 2323, fol. 67.*]

PLATE XII, No. 12. Bust to right of Giangaleazzo Visconti. Copied from a miniature?

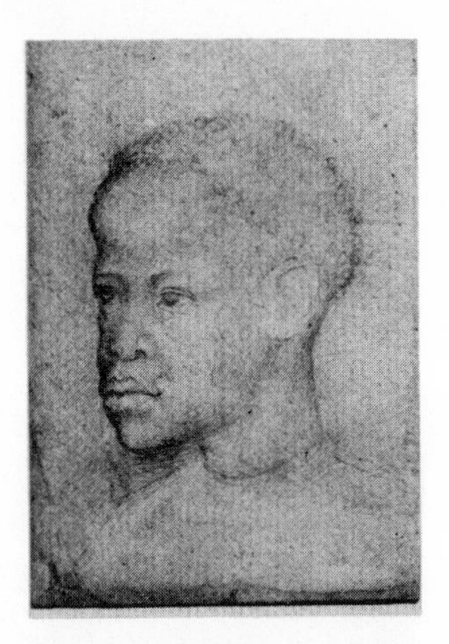

[*Louvre, Vallardi 2324, fol. 67.*]

PLATE XII, No. 13. Head of a young Negro, three-quarters to left.

[*Louvre, Vallardi 2321, fol. 66.*]

PLATE XII, No. 14. Head of a man in profile to right.

[*Louvre, Vallardi, 2314, fol. 63.*]

PLATE XII, No. 15. Profile to left of a man (? Borso d'Este).

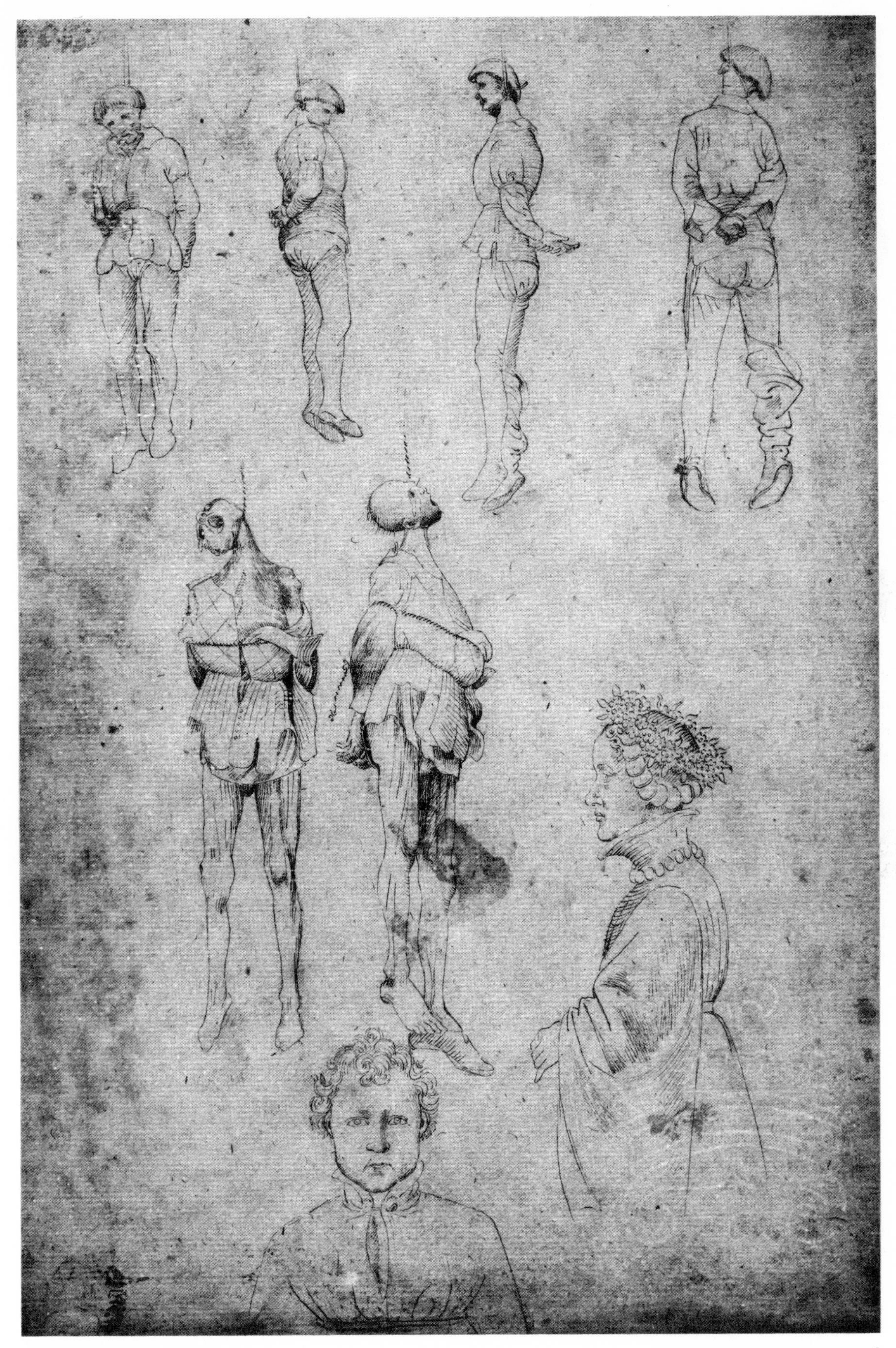

[*British Museum, 1895-9-15-441.*]

PLATE XIII, No. 16. Corpses hanging from gallows; bust of a boy facing, etc.

PLATE XIV, No. 17. Right profile of Princess of the South Anastasia fresco. [*Louvre, Vallardi, 2343, fol. 93.*]

[*Louvre, Vallardi* 2323, *fol.* 68.]

PLATE XV, No. 18. A Kalmuck archer and other studies.

[*Chantilly, Musée Condé.*]

PLATE XVI, No. 19. A courtier and a lady.

[*Louvre, Vallardi 2468, fol. 277.*]

PLATE XVII, No. 20. Two horses saddled and harnessed, one of them three-quarters to front, with slit nostrils, the other foreshortened from behind.

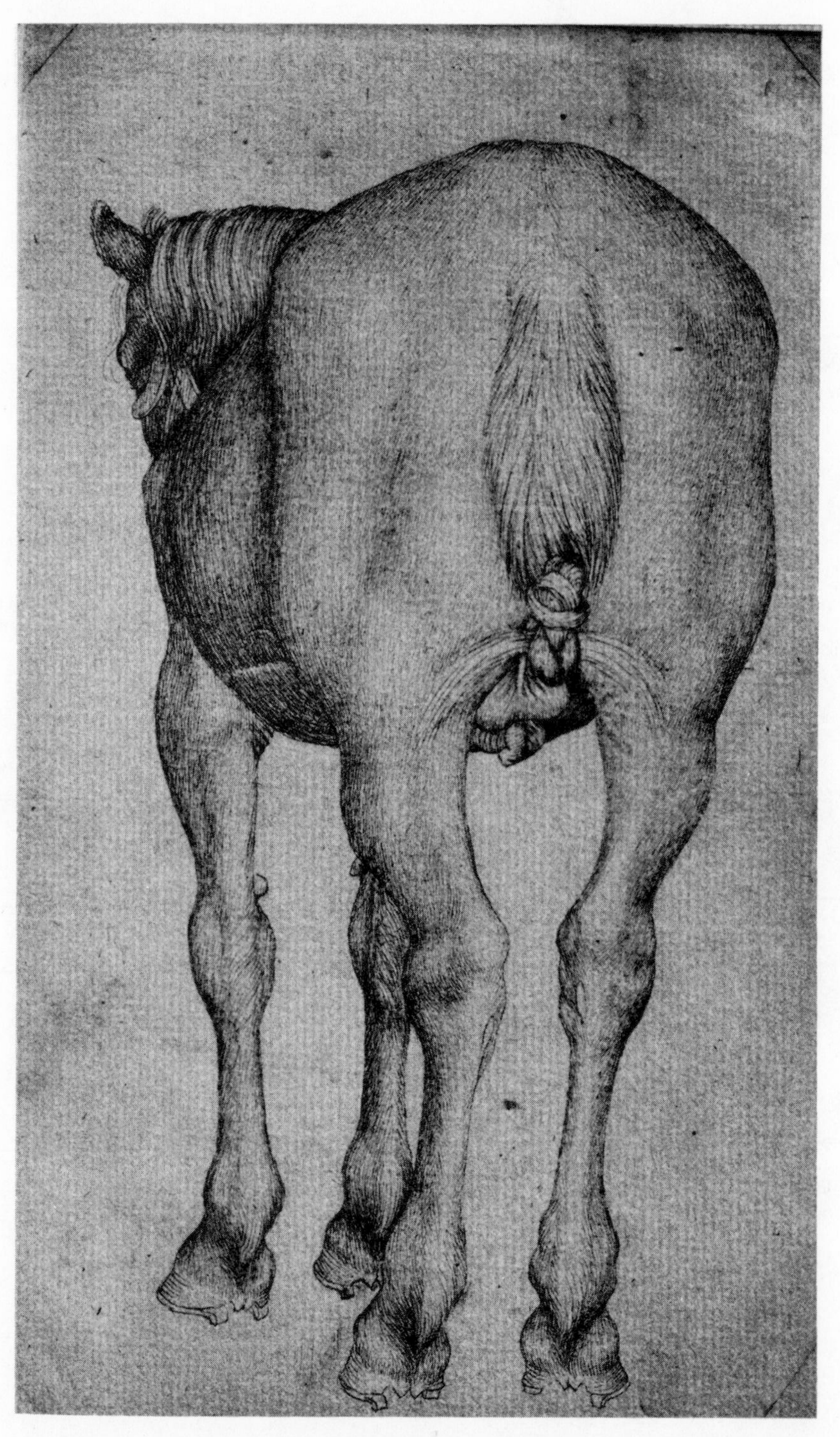

[*Louvre, Vallardi 2444, fol. 231.*]

PLATE XVIII, No. 21. A horse, foreshortened from behind, three-quarters to left, his tail tied up.

[*Louvre, Vallardi 2378, fol. 171.*]

PLATE XIX, No. 22. Saddled and harnessed horse, seen from behind, branded on the right hind haunch.

[*Louvre, Vallardi 2369, fol. 165.*]

PLATE XX, No. 23. Horse lying on its side to left, the off legs drawn up.

[*Louvre, Vallardi 2370, fol. 165.*]

PLATE XXI, No. 24. Horse lying on its side to left, all the legs extended.

[*Louvre, Vallardi 2405, fol. 198.*]

PLATE XXII, No. 26. Head of a horse with slit nostrils, pricking its ears, seen from the front.

[*Louvre, Vallardi 2455, fol. 267.*]

PLATE XXII, No. 25. Forepart of a horse; two studies of the mouth, and one of the eye.

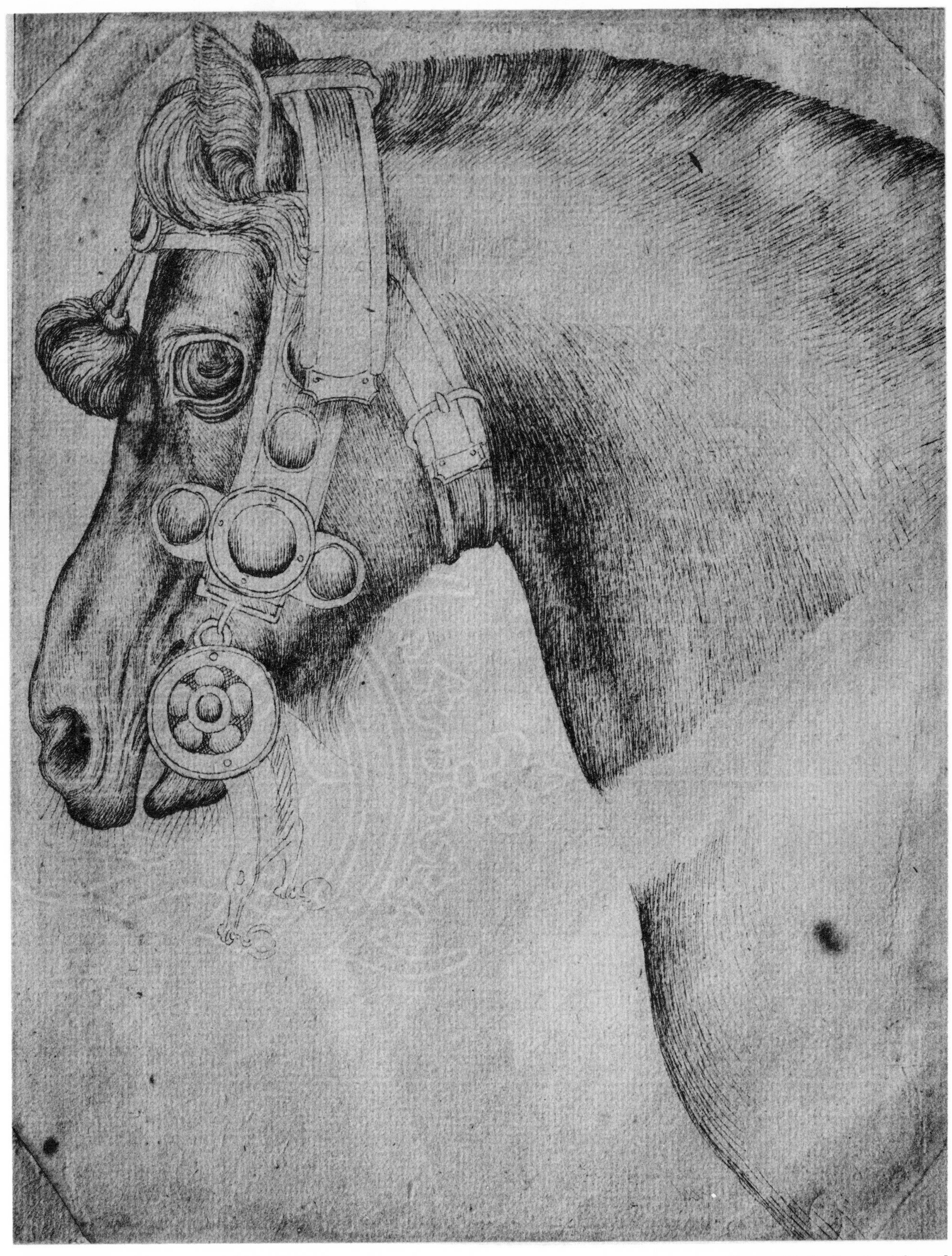

[*Louvre, Vallardi 2361, fol. 150.*]

PLATE XXIII, No. 27. Head of a horse in left profile, richly harnessed and bridled.

[*Louvre, Vallardi 2363, fol. 152.*]

PLATE XXIV, No. 28. Head of a haltered horse to right, turned slightly to front, with slit nostrils.

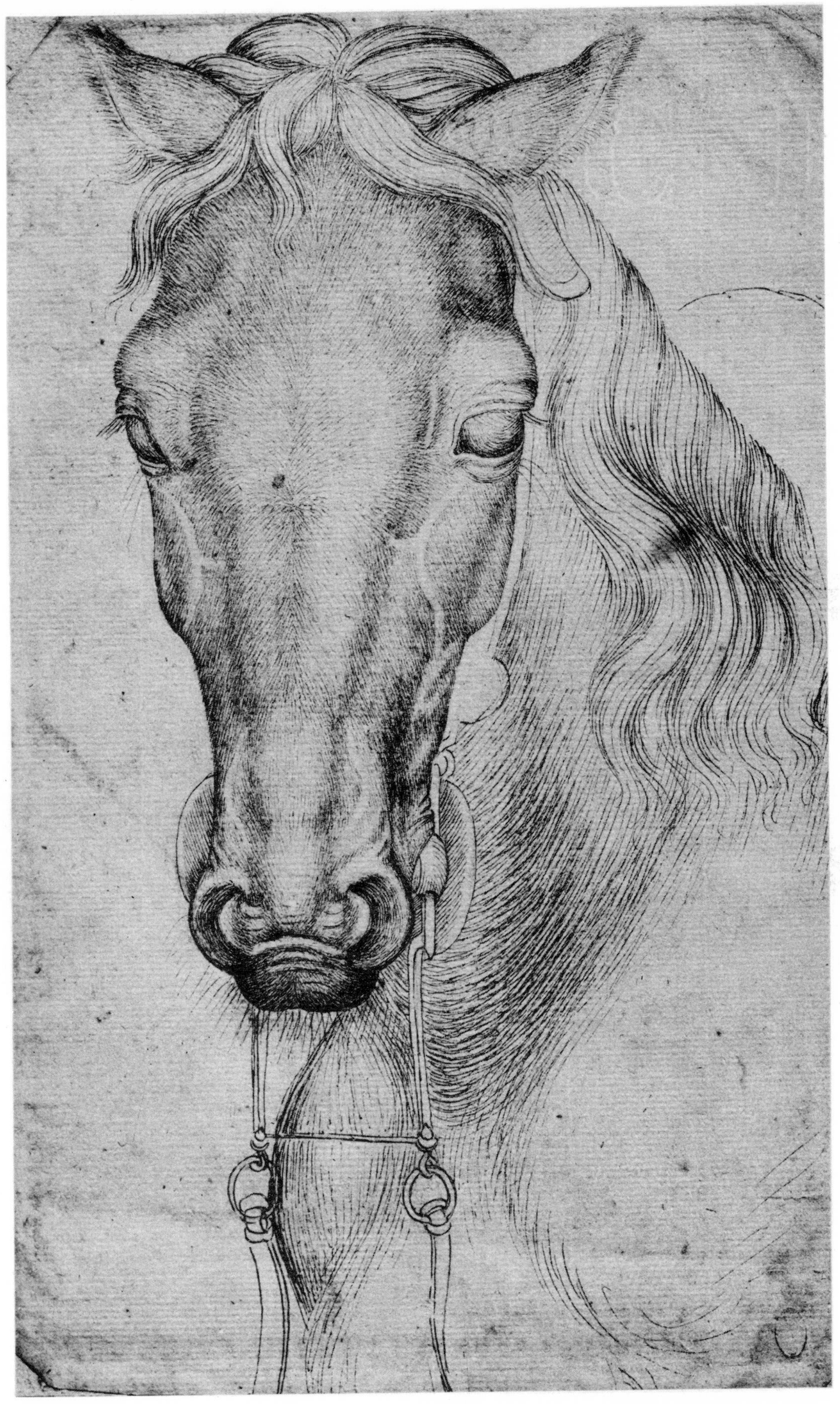

[*Louvre, Vallardi 2360, fol. 149.*]

PLATE XXV, No. 29. Head of horse to front, with hanging bridle.

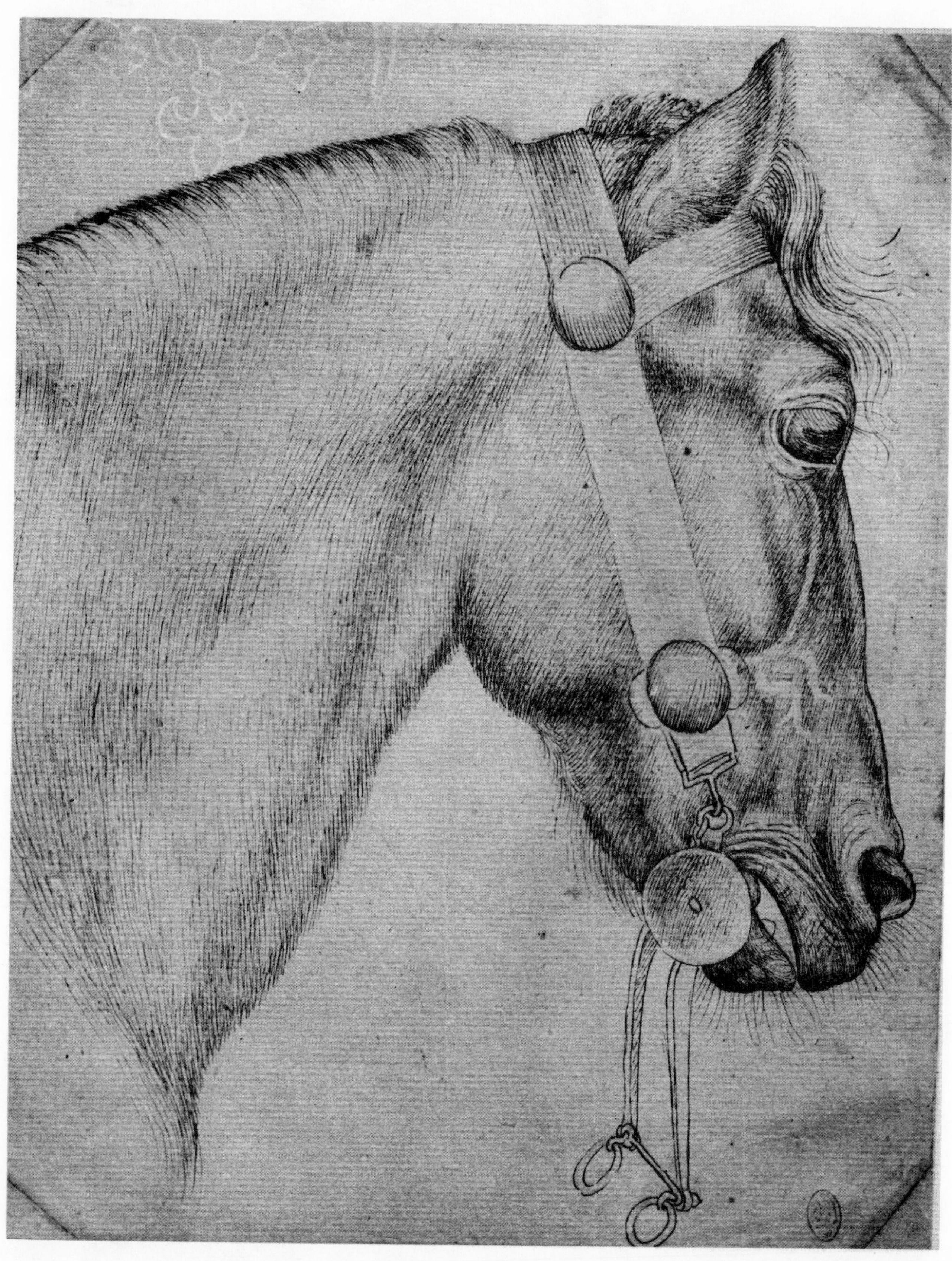

PLATE XXVI, No. 30. Head of horse to right, with hanging bridle. [*Louvre, Vallardi 2358, fol. 147.*]

[*Louvre, Vallardi 2357, fol. 146.*]

PLATE XXVII, No. 31. Head of horse to right, bridled.

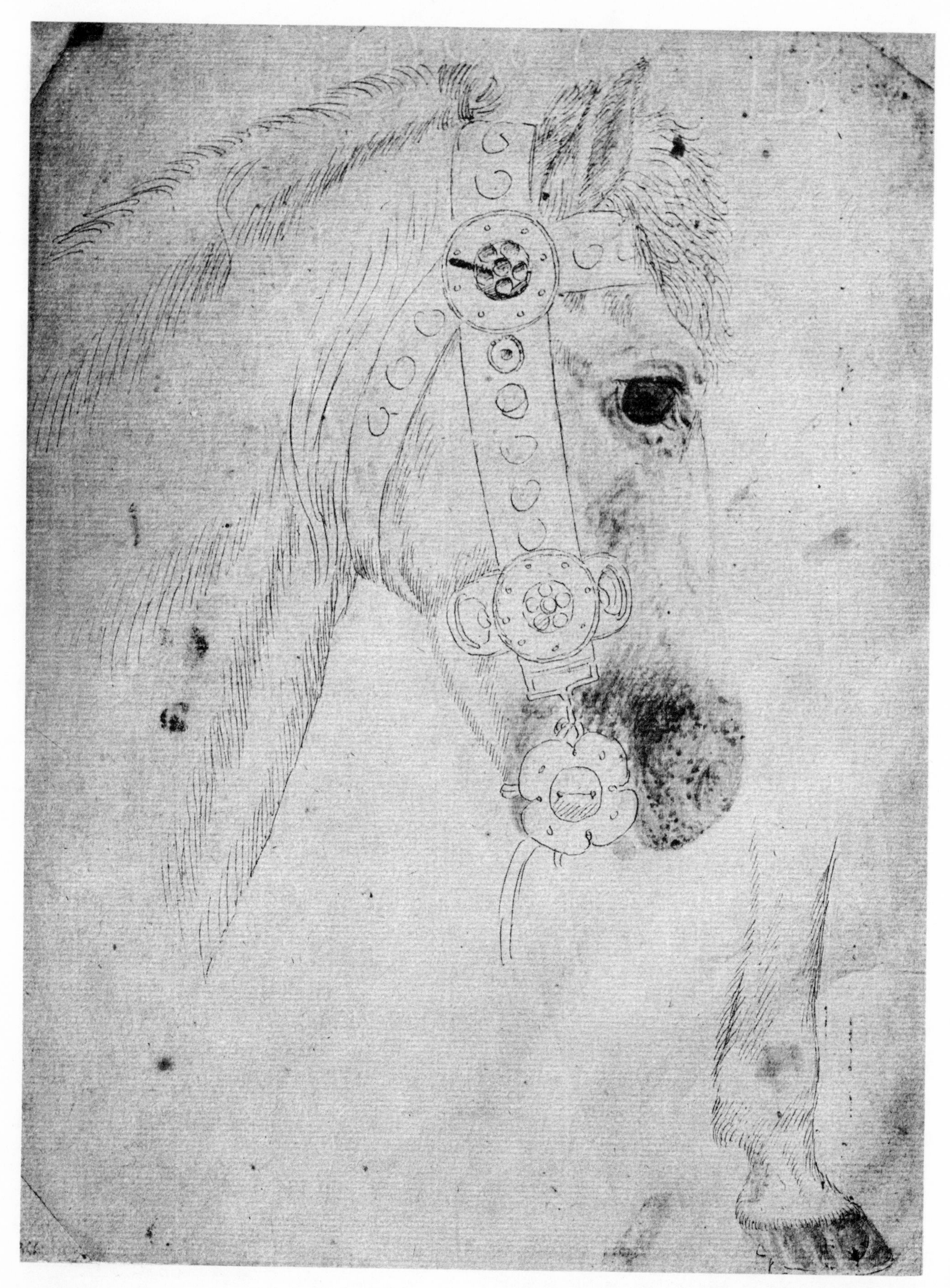

PLATE XXVIII, No. 32. Head of a bridled horse in profile to right, and a foreleg. [*Louvre, Vallardi 2356, fol. 145.*]

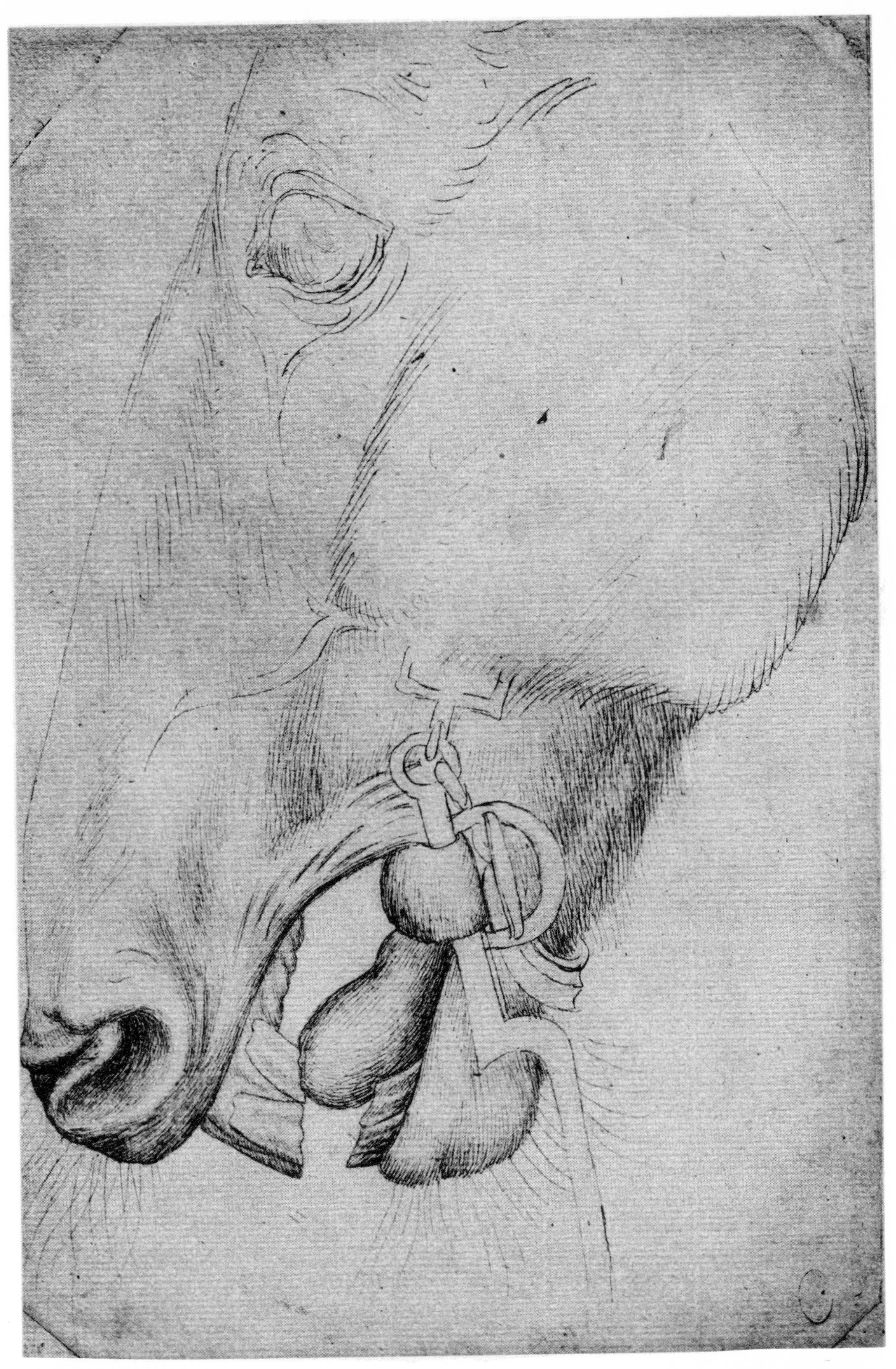

[*Louvre, Vallardi 2355, fol. 144.*]

PLATE XXIX, No. 33. Head of a bridled horse in left profile.

PLATE XXX, No. 34. Two studies of a horse's head, and one of the nose. [*Louvre, Vallardi 2354, fol. 143.*]

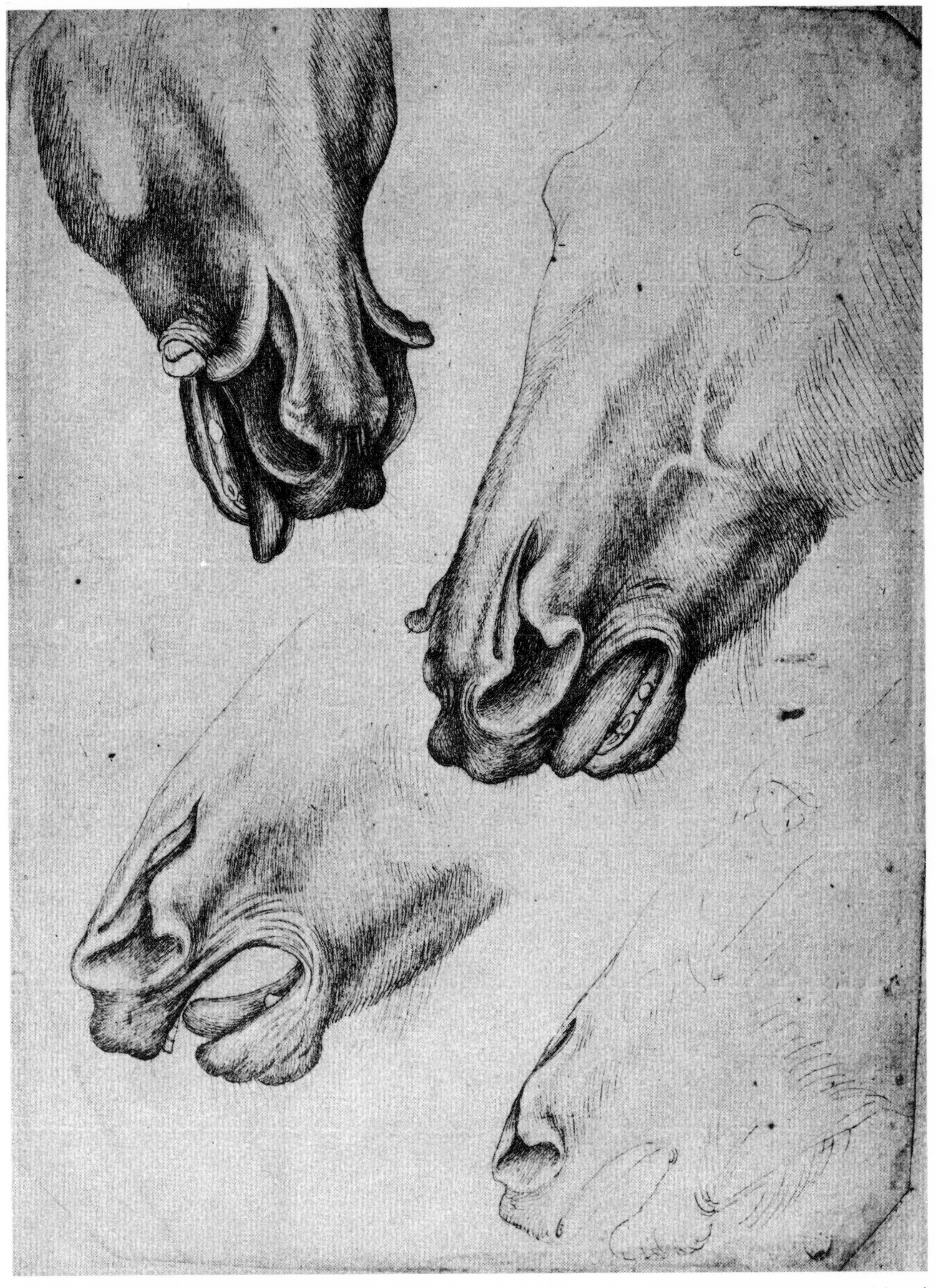

[*Louvre, Vallardi 2353, fol. 142.*]

PLATE XXXI, No. 35. Four studies of horses' muzzles, with slit nostrils.

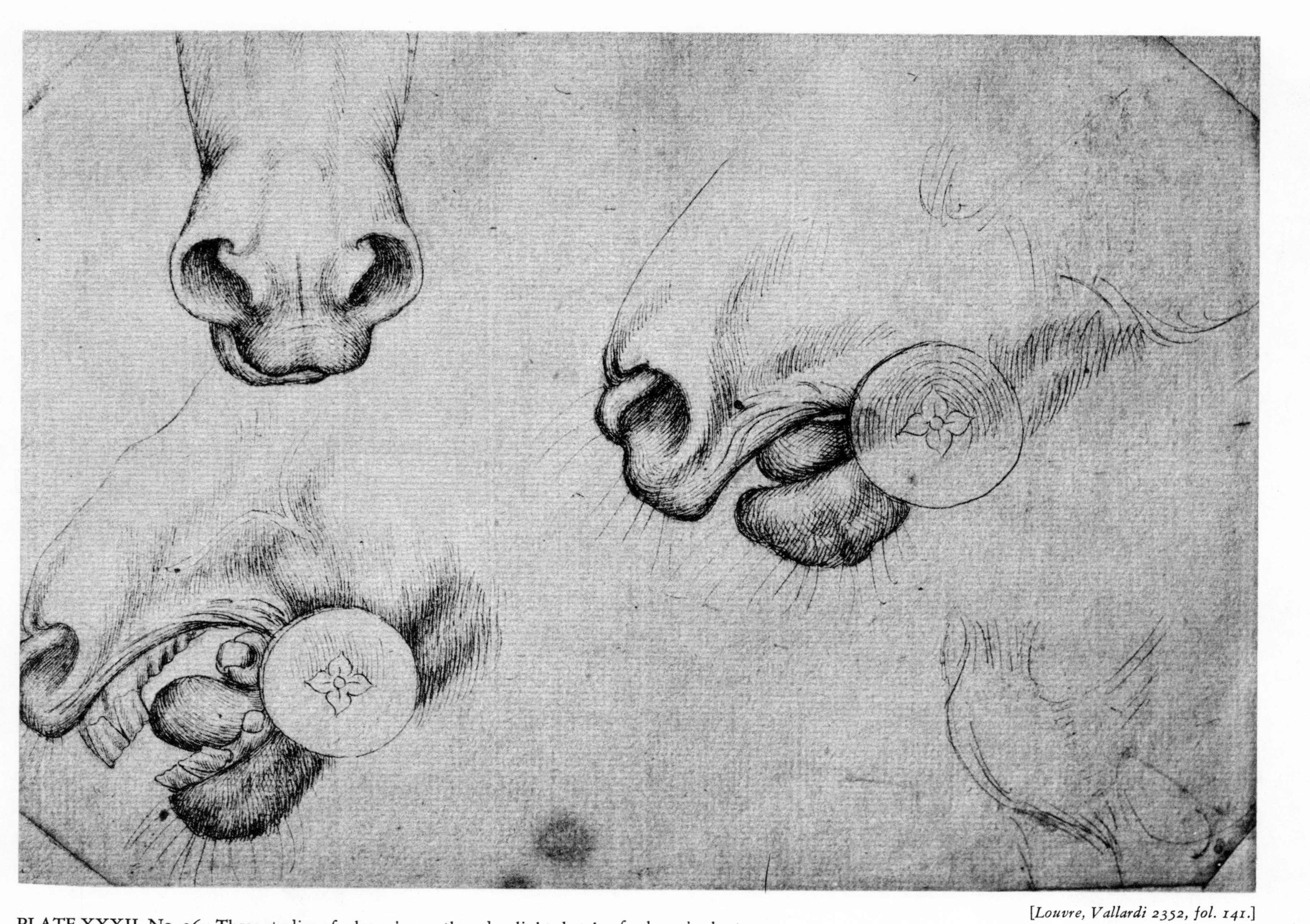

[*Louvre, Vallardi 2352, fol. 141.*]

PLATE XXXII, No. 36. Three studies of a horse's mouth and a slight sketch of a horse's chest.

[*Louvre, Vallardi 2380, fol. 174.*]

PLATE XXXIII, No. 37. Mule, saddled, harnessed and bitted, standing to left.

[*Louvre, Vallardi 2493, fol. 237.*]

PLATE XXXIV, No. 39. Captive chamois.

[*Louvre, Vallardi 2458, fol. 270.*]

PLATE XXXIV, No. 38. An ass standing to left, its ears laid back.

[*Louvre, Vallardi 2489, fol. 234.*]

PLATE XXXV, No. 40. A stag seen from behind, lying down to left, head turned away.

[*Louvre, Vallardi 2490, fol. 235.*]

PLATE XXXVI, No. 41. Two studies of the head of a stag and the head of a doe.

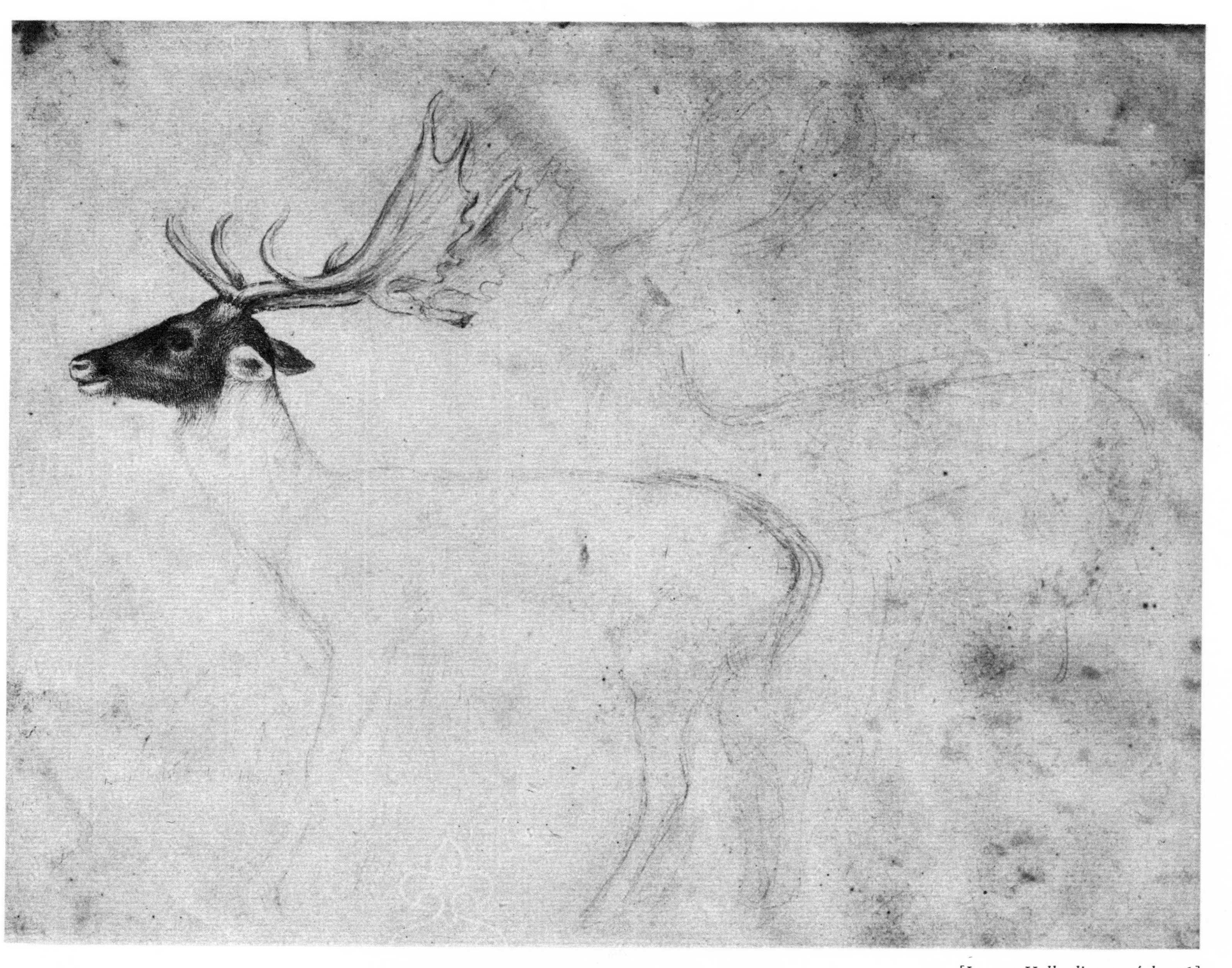

PLATE XXXVII, No. 42. A stag standing to left.

[*Louvre, Vallardi 2492, fol. 236.*]

[*Louvre, Vallardi 2494, fol. 237.*]

PLATE XXXVIII, No. 43. Two studies of a stag, one of its head, and two guinea-fowls.

[*Louvre, Vallardi 2497, fol. 242.*]

PLATE XXXVIII, No. 44. Young roebuck standing to right.

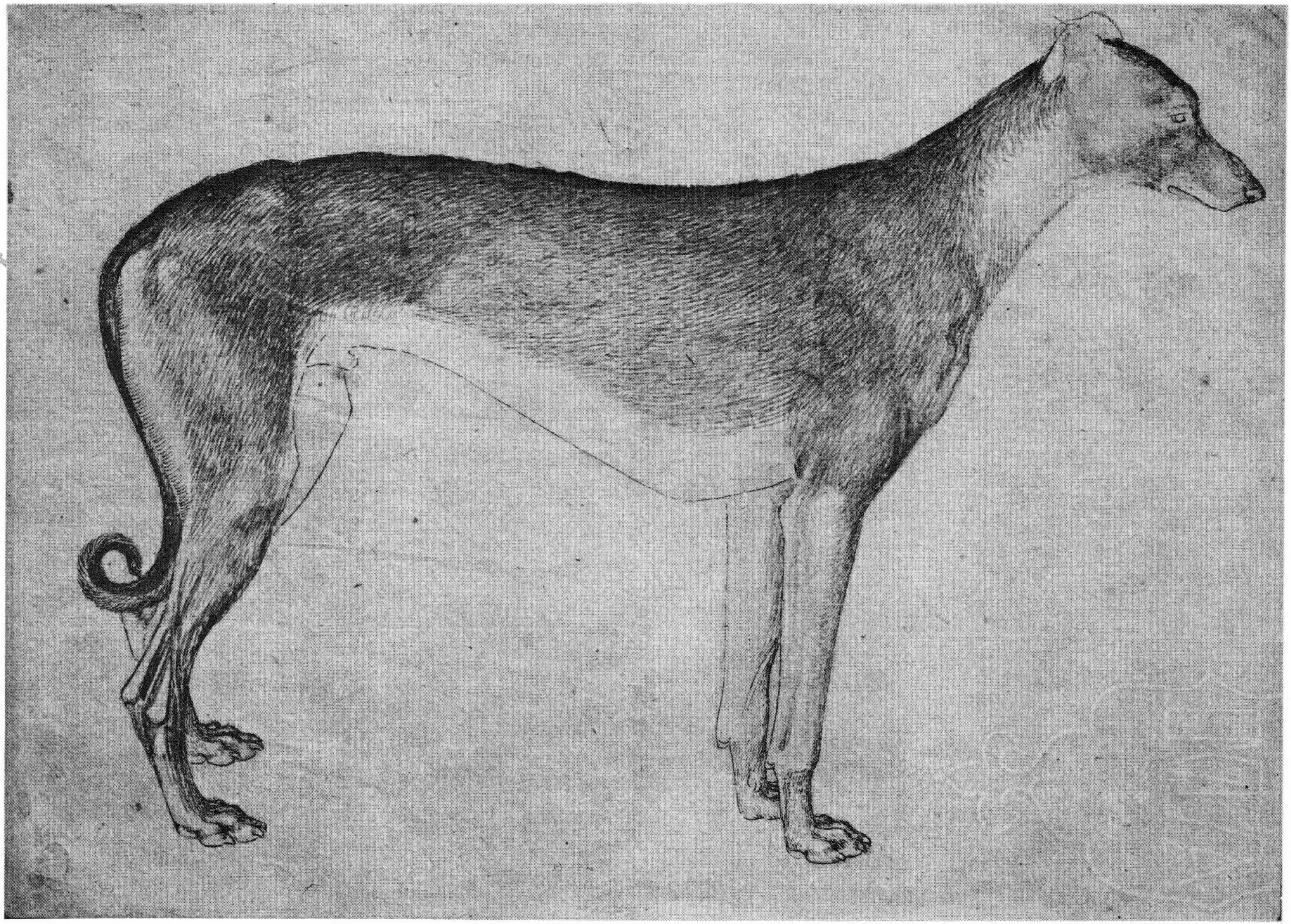

[*Louvre, Vallardi 2433, fol. 223.*]

PLATE XXXIX, No. 45. Greyhound standing to right.

[*Louvre, Vallardi* 2434, *fol.* 224.]

PLATE XL, No. 46. A greyhound, muzzled and collared, standing to left.

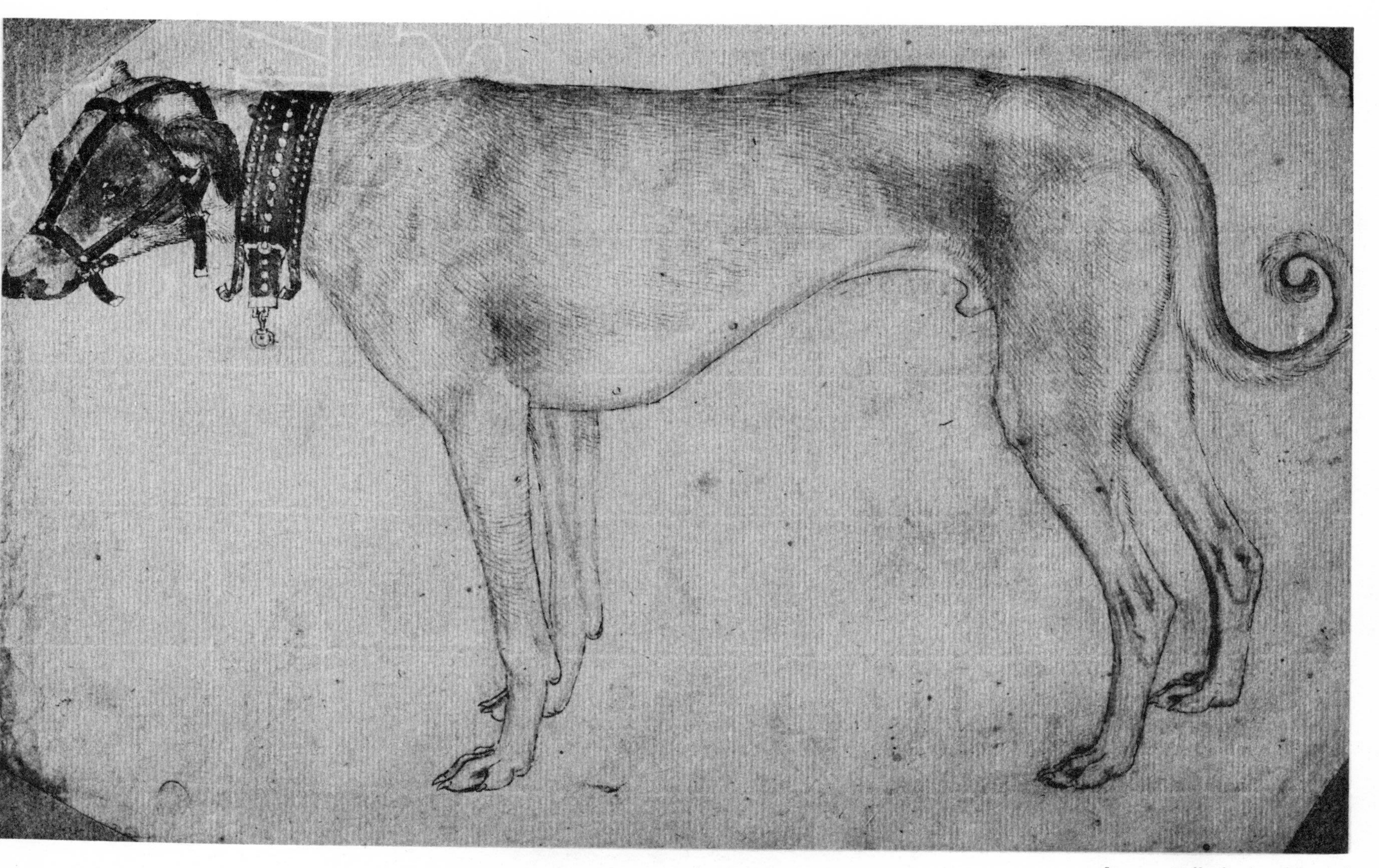

PLATE XLI, No. 47. A greyhound standing to left, wearing red collar and muzzle. [*Louvre, Vallardi 2435, fol. 225.*]

[Louvre, Vallardi 2430, fol. 221.]

PLATE XLII, No. 48. Head of a greyhound to right.

PLATE XLIII, No. 49. Head of a hound to right.

[*Louvre, Vallardi 2429, fol. 220.*]

[*Louvre, Vallardi 2423, fol. 215.*]

PLATE XLIV, No. 50. A fox lying to left.

[*Louvre, Vallardi 2424, fol. 215.*]

PLATE XLV, No. 51. A wolf standing to left.

PLATE XLVI, No. 52. A wolf or wild dog, seen from front, three-quarters to left. [*Louvre, Vallardi 2419, fol. 212.*]

[*Louvre, Vallardi 2425, fol. 216.*]

PLATE XLVII, No. 53. A cheetah; also three twisted columns.

[*Louvre, Vallardi 2426, fol. 216.*]

PLATE XLVIII, No. 54. A cheetah springing to right.

[*Louvre, Vallardi 2422, fol. 214.*]

PLATE XLIX, No. 55. A cat lying to left.

[*Louvre, Vallardi 2409, fol. 202.*]

PLATE L, No. 56. A pair of buffaloes, yoked, walking to left.

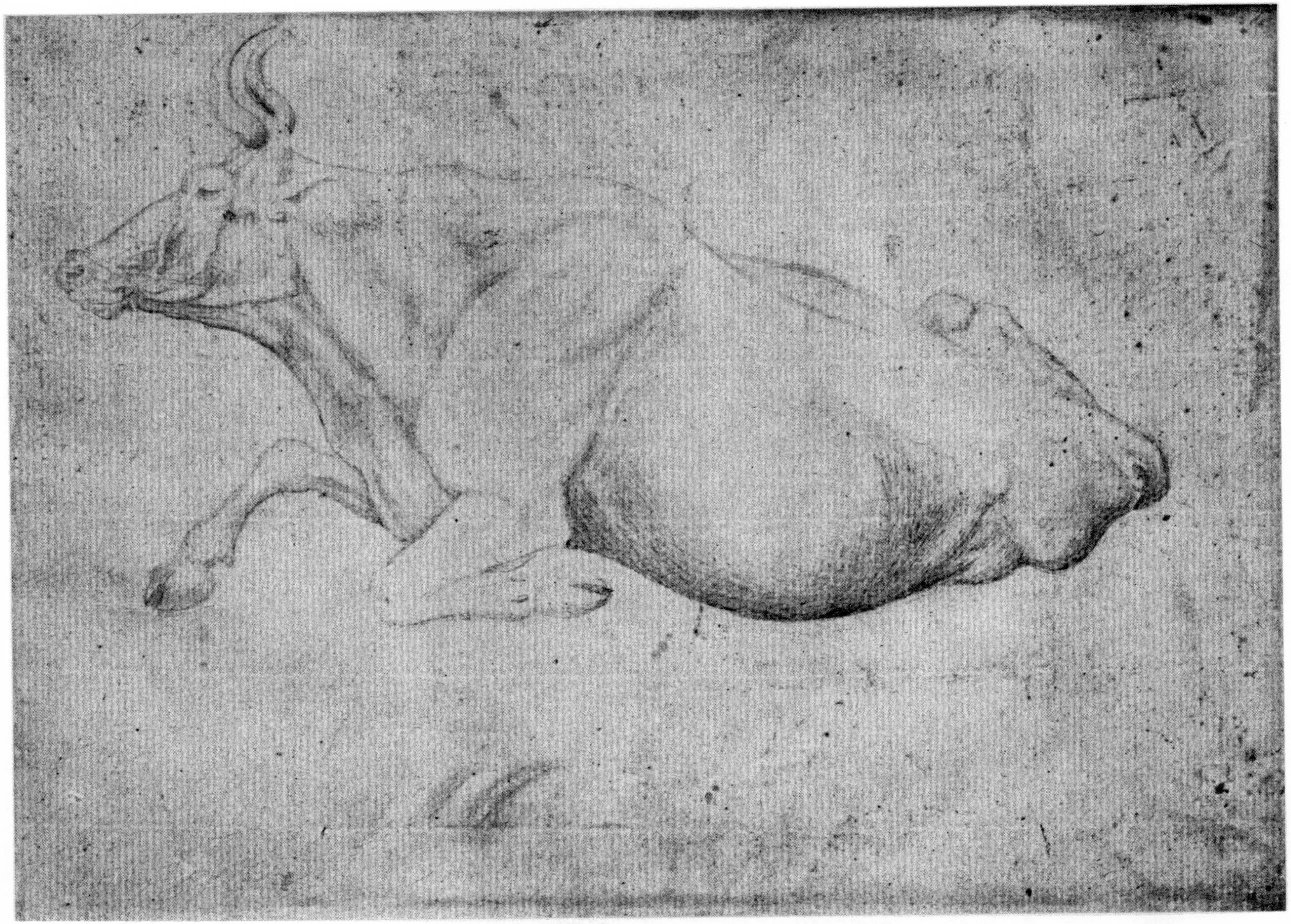

[*Louvre, Vallardi 2410, fol. 203.*]

PLATE LI, No. 57. Cow lying down to left, about to get up.

PLATE LII, No. 58. Three studies of oxen lying down.

[*Louvre, Vallardi 2411, fol. 204.*]

[*Louvre, Vallardi 2417, fol. 210.*]

PLATE LIII, No. 59. A boar standing to right.

[*Louvre, Vallardi 2485, fol. 258.*]

PLATE LIV, No. 60. Two studies of heraldic eagles.

[*Louvre, Vallardi 2452, fol. 265.*]

PLATE LV, No. 61. A falcon, seen from behind.

[*Louvre, Vallardi 2453, fol. 265.*]

PLATE LVI, No. 62. A falcon, with blue hood, seen from behind, perched on falconer's wrist.

[*Louvre, Vallardi 2450, fol. 263.*]

PLATE LVII, No. 64. An egret to right.

PLATE LVIII, No. 65. Two hoopoes.

[*Louvre, Vallardi 2467, fol. 276.*]

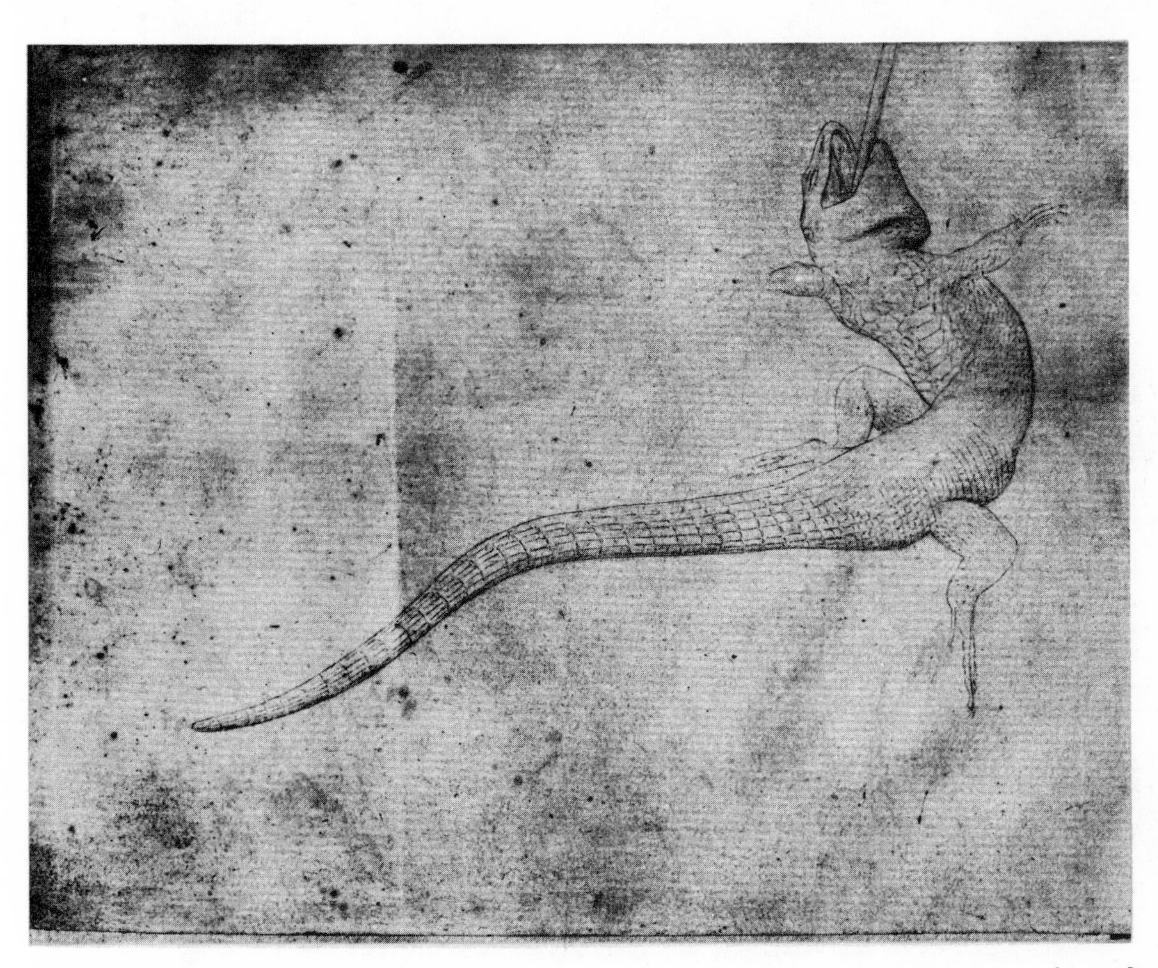

[Louvre, Vallardi 2382, fol. 179.]

PLATE LIX, No. 66. Lizard spitted through the mouth.

PLATE LX, No. 67. A lizard.

[Louvre, Vallardi 2383, fol. 179.]

[Louvre, Vallardi 2419, fol. 212 v.]

PLATE LXI, No. 68. Studies of flowers.

PLATE LXII, No. 69. Study for a medal of Alfonso of Aragon. [Louvre, Vallardi 2486, fol. 249.]

[Louvre, Vallardi 2307, fol. 61.]

PLATE LXIII, No. 70. Study for the 'Liberalitas' medal of Alfonso of Aragon.

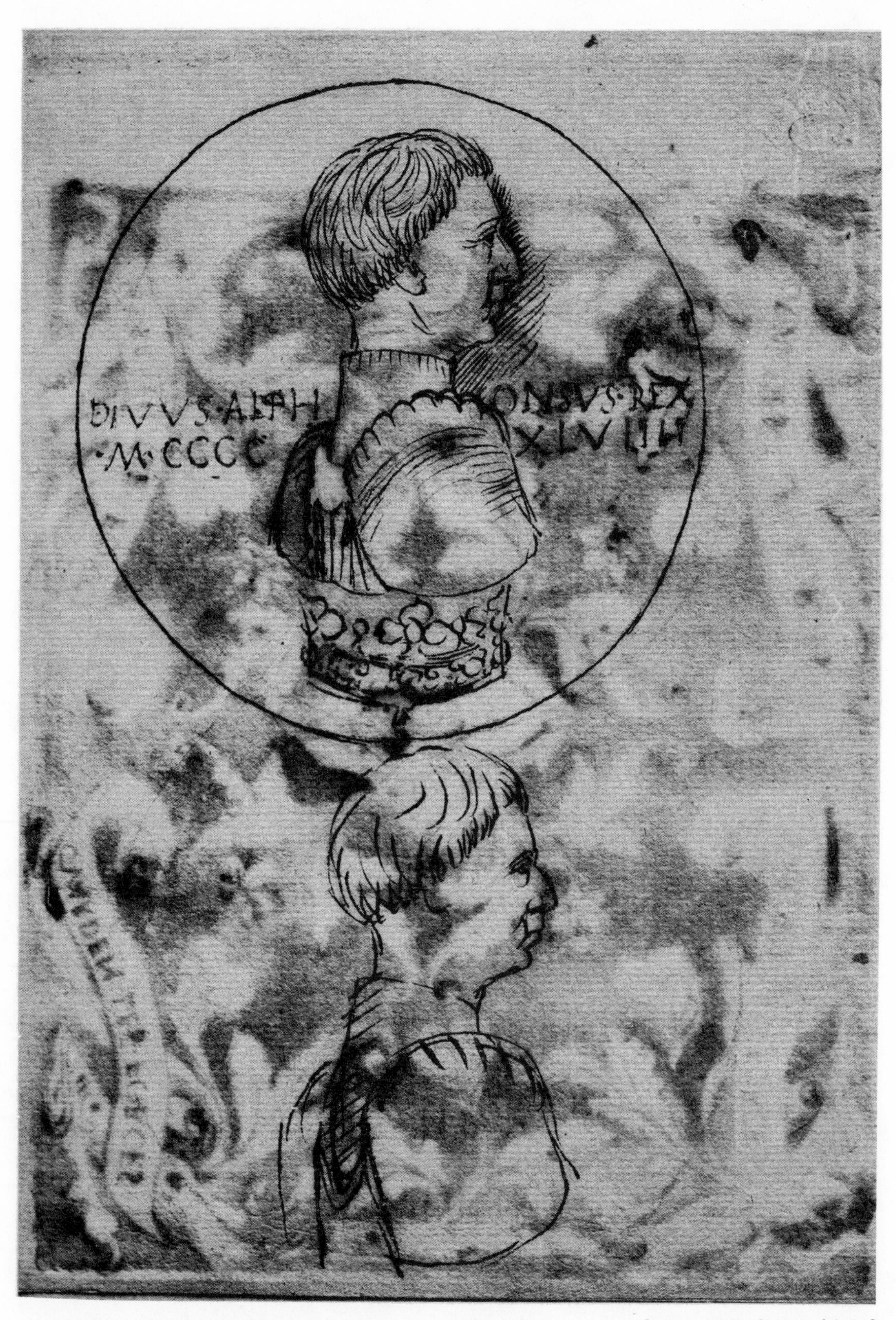

[Louvre, Vallardi 2306, fol. 61.]

PLATE LXIV, No. 71. Study for the 'Venator Intrepidus' medal of Alfonso of Aragon.